NO LA~~~~~~~~~K NEEDED!

Ever wonder if the Brady kids ever dated each other? In this wacky, revealing guide, you'll learn the answer to that and much more, including:

- The Bradys' phone number
- The episode in which the Brady Six musical group was born
- Which Brady cast member made a living recording Mattel doll voices before the show
- What network concern led to the addition of Carol's nephew Oliver to the family
- Why Susan Olsen hated her own character so much
- Amusing anecdotes and fun trivia about the show and its cast

A MUST-HAVE GUIDE FOR ALL BRADY BUNCH FANS!

Other TV Treasures Companion Guides

GILLIGAN'S ISLAND

TV TREASURES

A COMPANION GUIDE TO

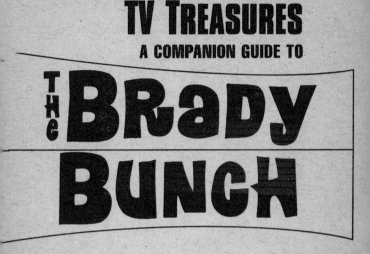

THE BRADY BUNCH

SYLVIA STODDARD

St. Martin's Paperbacks

Map to Clinton Way

THANKS

Tom Wilson generously provided access to his extensive collection of *Brady*-related material and was an inspiration. David E. Brady was also a great help with information and access to his collection, as was Lisa Sutton.

Kathy Clements, thanks to her diligence as a collector/dealer, made the photo section what it is, and the book wouldn't have been possible without the help of Donovan, Heidi and Claire Brandt at Eddie Brandt's Saturday Matinee in North Hollywood, a haven for classic TV lovers.

Thanks also to Janet Dubin, T. S. Lamb, Hamilton T. Bear and special thanks to my agent Ellen Geiger, and my friends, who are better than family.

WHY?

This is the question that launches nearly every interview with any cast member of *The Brady Bunch*. Why was the show such a hit? Why is it still on TV after a quarter of a century? What appeal does this idealized fluff, that was unrealistic even in 1969, have to anyone in the '90s?

The answers are clear. We all wanted a family like the Bradys. If we were only children, we wished we had a brother like Greg or a sister like Marcia. Even if we had siblings, we wished they were more like Bobby or Jan or Peter or Cindy. Who wouldn't have loved parents who dropped everything when you had a problem—even one as inconsequential as a pesky math problem?

The show was a wacky sort of proof that even in the confusing and chaotic '70s, it still might be possible to shut out reality as soon as we crossed the threshold of our split-level suburban ranch houses.

But mostly, *The Brady Bunch* was a show for kids, detailing the everyday problems that loomed so large in their own lives: school, braces, dating, puberty, cars, friendships, and homework. Television programming in 1969 was designed primarily to attract adult viewers; the only thing on TV for younger viewers were cartoons, which were considered "kid stuff" by anyone the age of most of the Brady kids.

With the creation of *The Brady Bunch* and *Gilligan's Island*, Sherwood Schwartz contributed one thing to all our lives: He offered two shows that focused on getting along with each other. In a world obsessed with the Cold War, this was potent stuff. No more disparate souls existed than the "seven castaways," and conflict was guaranteed, just as it is in the real world. The Bradys were also two warring nations forced into an uneasy alliance. The lesson was sugar-coated and disguised, but both shows sure gave us a model for getting along: compromise and sharing. Maybe all of Dad Brady's morals seeped into our subconscious minds and made us better people. We can only hope so.

But if you're still wondering why *The Brady Bunch* is such a phenomenon, read on.

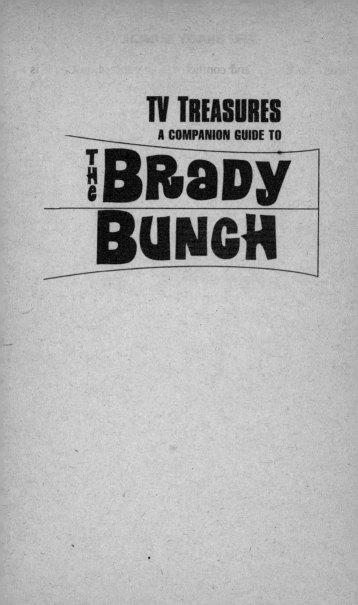

TV TREASURES

A COMPANION GUIDE TO

The BRady BUNCH

THE FIRST SEASON

1969–1970

FRIDAY NIGHTS—FALL 1969

	ABC	CBS	NBC
7:30	Let's Make a Deal	Get Smart	The High Chaparral
8:00	THE BRADY BUNCH	The Good Guys	
8:30	Mr. Deeds Goes to Town	Hogan's Heroes	The Name of the Game
9:00	Here Come the Brides	CBS Friday Night Movie	
9:30			
10:00	The Lennon Sisters		Bracken's World
10:30			

FRIDAY NIGHTS—WINTER 1969–70

	ABC	CBS	NBC
7:30	The Flying Nun	Get Smart	The High Chaparral
8:00	THE BRADY BUNCH	The Tim Conway Show	
8:30	The Ghost and Mrs. Muir	Hogan's Heroes	The Name of the Game
9:00	Here Come the Brides	CBS Friday Night Movie	
9:30			
10:00	Love, American Style		Bracken's World
10:30			

SEASON RATINGS*
October 1969–April 1970

1.	Rowan & Martin's Laugh-In	26.3
2.	Gunsmoke	25.9
3.	Bonanza	24.8
4.	Mayberry R.F.D.	24.4
5.	Family Affair	24.2
6.	Here's Lucy	23.9
7.	The Red Skelton Hour	23.8
8.	Marcus Welby, M.D.	23.7
9.	Walt Disney's Wonderful World of Color	23.6
10.	The Doris Day Show	22.8
11.	The Bill Cosby Show	22.7
12.	The Jim Nabors Hour	22.4
13.	The Carol Burnett Show	22.1
14.	The Dean Martin Show	21.9
15.	My Three Sons	21.8
	Ironside	21.8
	The Johnny Cash Show	21.8
18.	The Beverly Hillbillies	21.7
19.	Hawaii Five-O	21.1
20.	The Glen Campbell Goodtime Hour	21.0
	Hee Haw	21.0
22.	Movie of the Week	20.9
23.	The Mod Squad	20.8
24.	Saturday Night Movie	20.6
	Bewitched	20.6
	The F.B.I.	20.6

*Ratings represent the percentage of all TV-equipped households watching this particular show. Thus, an average of 26.3% of all homes with televisions were tuned to *Rowan & Martin's Laugh-In* per week during the season.

THE WORLD
1969

- Astronaut Neil Armstrong took man's first step on the moon, while 500 million people watched on their television sets.
- The New York Jets won the Super Bowl, the New York Mets had an incredible season, then stunned everyone by wiping out the Baltimore Orioles in the World Series in five games.
- The *Saturday Evening Post* ceased publication after 148 years.
- Mary Jo Kopechne drowned in Senator Ted Kennedy's car on Chappaquiddick.
- Clay L. Shaw was acquitted in New Orleans of conspiring to assassinate President John F. Kennedy.
- The Concorde, a supersonic passenger jetliner, made its first test flight to France.
- Sirhan Bishara Sirhan was convicted of assassinating Senator Robert F. Kennedy in Los Angeles.
- Miniskirts were on the way out, maxicoats, skirts, vests, and sweaters were on the way in. Pantsuits (called "trouser outfits") were finally considered acceptable dress for women.
- In movies, big-budget, sure-fire films failed (such as Julie Andrews's portrayal of Gertrude Lawrence in *Star!* and Vanessa Redgrave in *Isadora*) and low-budget offbeat films were huge hits (*The Graduate, The Wild Bunch, Midnight Cowboy, Bonnie and Clyde*). *Oliver!*

was voted Best Picture by the Motion Picture Academy, and Katharine Hepburn (*The Lion in Winter*) and Barbra Streisand (*Funny Girl*) tied for Best Actress.

- In mid-November a "March Against Death" was staged in Washington, with 46,000 people attending and each carrying the name of a soldier killed in Vietnam. The crowd swelled to 250,000 the next day.

- The Roman Catholic Church eliminated over 200 saints in its new liturgical calendar.

- The prime interest rate was raised from 7½ to 8½ percent.

- In its fifteenth year, rock music had changed and so had the big groups. Graham Nash left the Hollies, the Bee Gees became a group of three instead of five, Brian Jones left the Rolling Stones (and then died in a freak drowning accident several weeks later), and several groups broke up altogether (Traffic, Cream, Family). A new type of rock—slow, simple, and loud—began to be called "heavy rock." John Lennon married Yoko Ono, the Beatles released *Abbey Road*, and there were widespread stories that Paul McCartney was dead (he wasn't). Beatles protégé Mary Hopkin had a huge hit with "Those Were the Days."

- President Nixon made a trip to Southeast Asia to explain he was not abandoning the area though he was withdrawing troops.

- Vice President Agnew accused the three television networks of slanting the news. Several days later, he made similar charges against the press. This signaled the start of the media's investigation of political sacred cows which would culminate in Watergate.

- On and Off-Broadway, actors took off their clothes (*Oh! Calcutta!, Ché!, Sweet Eros*) and put on wigs (*1776*). Popular musicals included *Zorba* and *Promises, Promises*. Dustin Hoffman starred in *Jimmy Shine* and Julie Harris in *Forty Carats*. Regional theater contributed a fine play to Broadway, *The Great White Hope*.

- The Gulf Coast was devastated by hurricane Camille,

which killed over 400 people and caused $1 billion in damage.
- Capital punishment was abolished in the U.K.
- Cyclamates, the most popular and widely used artificial sweeteners in the U.S., were banned after tests showed they caused cancer and birth defects in laboratory animals.

TELEVISION
1969

- The big television event of the year was the moonwalk, which was broadcast all over the world.
- The Smothers Brothers were testing the limits of censorship with CBS, and refused to make their programs available for review prior to airing. They were thrown off the air.
- There were significantly more black actors in prime-time shows than previous years, including leads in *The Mod Squad, Julia, Ironside, The Leslie Uggams Show, Room 222, Mannix, The Bold Ones, The Bill Cosby Show, The New People, Love, American Style,* and *Rowan & Martin's Laugh-In.*
- *Peyton Place* went off the air, and doctor shows were back, with the premieres of *Marcus Welby, M.D., Medical Center,* and *The Doctors.*
- *Sesame Street,* a bold new experiment in preschool children's programming, premiered on PBS.

- The marriage of Tiny Tim (wavery-voiced singer of the hit record "Tip Toe Through the Tulips") and Miss Vicki on *The Tonight Show* registered the highest audience numbers ever for a late-night show.
- On *My Three Sons*, widower Fred MacMurray married Beverly Garland. *I Dream of Jeannie's* Barbara Eden wed Jeannie's Major Nelson, played by Larry Hagman.
- *Bewitched's* Samantha (Elizabeth Montgomery) had her second child and Dick Sargent replaced Dick York as Darrin Stephens. Agent 99 (Barbara Feldon) on *Get Smart* also got a visit from the stork, bringing twins.
- Fred Astaire joined the cast of *It Takes a Thief* as Alexander Mundy's (Robert Wagner) father. Barbara Bain and Martin Landau left *Mission: Impossible* after salary and billing disputes, and Leonard Nimoy joined the show as Paris.

THE BRADY BUNCH
1969

The Brady Bunch was ridiculed, dismissed, or ignored right from the start. *TV Guide* didn't seem to think much of *The Brady Bunch*. In the 1969 Fall Preview issue, a full page is devoted to each of the season's 29 new shows except for three: *Mr. Deeds Goes to Town*, *To Rome With Love*, and *The Brady Bunch*. In fact, the synopsis of the

Brady show's pilot is dismissive and rather patronizing.*

The lineup for Friday night on ABC was pretty weak, too. *Let's Make a Deal* was a game show transplanted from daytime. *Mr. Deeds Goes to Town* starred Monte Markham in a weak remake of an old Gary Cooper film and was gone by January. *Here Come the Brides* was a two-season minor hit that survived on the presence of teen idol Bobby Sherman. The full title of the final show of the night was *Jimmy Durante Presents the Lennon Sisters*, and was a creaky vaudeville-style variety show. It was moved to Saturday nights in January, and canceled in April.

For the second half of the season, *The Brady Bunch* was surrounded with much better shows and the entire night on ABC was designed to appeal to the same audience. *The Flying Nun* was exactly the same kind of fun, escapist comedy as *The Brady Bunch*, as were *The Ghost and Mrs. Muir* and *Love, American Style*.

Friday nights are traditionally low-viewing nights, and you'll note none of the Friday night shows are in the top 25 shows for the season. The race was tight—with only fractional differences in the ratings of the last ten shows on the chart.

---

*Incidentally, when the review says that the Bradys must coexist with no help from U Thant, it refers to the secretary-general of the United Nations at the time. The diplomat from Burma became head of the UN upon the death of Dag Hammarskjöld in 1961 and was re-elected for several four-year terms. He decried violence and focused his energies on the conflicts in the Middle East and Vietnam.

THE EPISODES

Television was finally beginning to acknowledge that the world's families weren't all like the Andersons (of *Father Knows Best*), the Nelsons (*The Adventures of Ozzie & Harriet*) or the Stones (*The Donna Reed Show*). Forget that few—if any—families ever were. But as the '70s dawned, some reflection on the upheaval of the '60s was deemed appropriate. And, as it had for decades, television reacted to what were hits in movie theaters.

Birth-control advances precluded the large nuclear families of previous generations, so the way to get the wacky interaction fostered by a big group was to put two families together. Debbie Reynolds adopted six orphans in 1963's *My Six Loves*, and then 1968 saw the release of *With Six You Get Eggroll*, a hit movie starring Doris Day and Brian Keith as a widow and widower with lots of kids. That same year, Henry Fonda and Lucille Ball starred in a similar comedy, *Yours, Mine and Ours*.

According to Andrew J. Edelstein and France Lovece's *The Brady Bunch Book*, someone at ABC remembered a pilot pitched some time before by *Gilligan's Island*'s creator Sherwood Schwartz, then titled *Yours and Mine*. ABC bought the show and Schwartz changed the title of his work (though his was created first) to *The Brady Bunch*. Schwartz then turned to the details of setting up a production team for the series. He brought in John Rich, who had directed the first few episodes of *Gilligan's Island*, to guide the character development in the first episodes.

Mike's profession isn't made clear in the pilot episode, so the Brady house is a very modern white one-story building. (Imagine *The Brady Bunch* without that staircase.) Since Mike Brady was an architect, Schwartz chose a custom-designed Studio City house that had all the requisites for a television location: it was located at the end of a dead end street, so it could be shot from a variety of angles; it had a large frontage on the street; it was quite different from the surrounding houses; and the neighborhood was quiet. The house wasn't large enough for eight, so the set designers hung a fake window on the high A-frame façade to make the house look like a two-story residence.

Then came casting. The six kids were the first order of business, and it was as difficult as you'd think to come up with three girls and three boys who resembled each other, who were also about the same ages.

Robert Reed was an early choice for Mike Brady, but Joyce Bulifant (Marie Slaughter, Murray's wife, on *The Mary Tyler Moore Show*) was the original choice for Carol, who was going to be the wacky wife character on the show. When she dropped out and Florence Henderson was cast, the comedic focus shifted to the housekeeper, Alice, and Ann B. Davis (famous for her role as Shultzy on *The Bob Cummings Show*) was a natural for the part.

1. PILOT—"THE HONEYMOON"
September 26, 1969
Written by Sherwood Schwartz
Directed by John Rich
Regulars: Robert Reed, Florence Henderson, Ann B. Davis, Maureen McCormick, Eve Plumb, Susan Olsen, Barry Williams, Christopher Knight, Mike Lookinland
Guests: J. Pat O'Malley............................Mr. Tyler
Joan Tompkins ....Mrs. Tyler
Dabbs Greer ....Minister
James Millhollin...........................Pringle

The future conflicts are clear as Michael Paul Brady and Carol Ann Tyler Martin prepare their families to be joined. The Brady boys insist upon taking their dog, Tiger, to the wedding, as he's a member of the family. This causes a problem with the Martin family cat, Fluffy, so Mike has the boys put their dog in the car.

The wedding is a lavish one, and takes place in the garden of the palatial Tyler home. All is well until the minister pronounces them man and wife and Fluffy meows. This prompts Tiger to work the power window in the car [TV magic, since the hand crank is clearly visible in the shot], jump out, and create complete havoc with a real cat and dog chase.

        ❁

You will, of course, notice that the sets for the Brady house are different in this pilot . The print currently being used by TBS makes the Brady kitchen look mauve, olive, and taxicab yellow with orange and black accessories. The '60s were wild, but not quite this bilious.

Presumably, Carol, Marcia, Jan, and Cindy lived with her parents, the Tylers, and Fluffy (the cat) stayed there, since Fluffy was never mentioned again.

Note two relics of the times in this pilot: Carol suggests with all seriousness that Mike take several tranquilizers; and, the word "obey" is still part of their exchanged marriage vows.

Barry Williams, in his book Growing Up Brady, *remembers, "We shot this pilot almost a full year before our first real episode," which explains why the kids are so much smaller here than in the rest of the season.*

Just as the network would refuse to let Mary Tyler Moore be a divorcée the next year, the network put the kibosh on Sherwood Schwartz's intention that Carol Martin be divorced. In retaliation, Schwartz never had her or the girls refer to their father, dead or otherwise. The deceased Brady mother is discussed though, and her photo is shown in the pilot.

J. Pat O'Malley, who plays Carol's father, was a regular on My Favorite Martian, Wendy and Me, The Rounders, A

Touch of Grace *and* Maude. *Joan Tompkins, who plays Carol's mother, also starred on* Occasional Wife *and* Sam Benedict. *Dabbs Greer is a veteran of many, many TV shows and costarred in* Gunsmoke, Hank *and* Little House on the Prairie. *James Millhollin is also a veteran of many shows, and was a regular on* Grindl.

2. "DEAR LIBBY"
October 3, 1969
Written by Lois Hire
Directed by John Rich
Regulars: Reed, Henderson, Davis, McCormick, Plumb, Olsen, Williams, Knight, Lookinland
Guest: Jo de Winter as.........................Dear Libby

There's something in the newspaper Marcia doesn't want her parents to see, so she removes the incriminating page. When they notice and Mike is about to go get another one, Marcia quickly volunteers and Mike sends Greg with her. Outside the house, Marcia shows Greg the offending article, a "Dear Libby" advice column with a letter from someone who has three kids, who has recently married someone else with three kids, and he or she finds they can't love the new members of the family. Marcia's sure it's from their mom or dad. They spill ink on the article in the new copy of the paper. Carol and Mike are suspicious, but can't figure what's going on.

The kids all have a meeting and decide the best way to make the offending spouse love the three adopted kids is to be on their best behavior. They go to great lengths to make the Brady home one of harmony and happiness. Carol and Mike get more and more suspicious. And so does Alice. She finally convinces Marcia and Greg to go to their folks. The boys talk to Mike and the girls to Carol, which results in Carol and Mike each thinking the other wrote the letter.

✿

Of course, the advice column "Dear Libby" is patterned after the "Dear Abby" column written for decades by Abigail Van Buren, and syndicated in newspapers all over the country.

3. "EENIE, MEENIE, MOMMY, DADDY"
October 10, 1969
Written by Joanna Lee
Directed by John Rich
Regulars: Reed, Henderson, Davis, McCormick, Plumb, Olsen, Williams, Knight, Lookinland
Guests: Marjorie Stapp as . . . . Mrs. Engstrom
            Tracy Reed as . . . . Miss Marlowe
            Brian Forster as . . . . The Elf

Cindy's thrilled to be chosen to play the fairy princess in the school play. Cindy works like a trooper to learn her part and practice the hard stunts for the show, and the whole family helps. But there's trouble at school. There aren't enough seats for all the parents of the participants to attend, and each student will be limited to receiving one ticket. Alice gives Cindy the bad news, and Cindy has to make a blindfolded choice. She picks the card marked "Dad," and is miserable. Her mother has always come to her school events.

All her brothers and sisters work so hard to help her that Cindy starts to feel guilty that they can't come see her either.

❀

Brian Forster (The Elf) played Chris on the next season's family comedy, The Partridge Family.

Robert Reed starred in Neil Simon's Barefoot in the Park *on Broadway, and originally came to Hollywood to star in a sitcom based on the play. The idea was shelved but revived some years later and starred Tracy Reed, who plays Miss Marlowe in this episode.*

4. "ALICE DOESN'T LIVE HERE ANYMORE"
October 17, 1969
Written by Paul West
Directed by John Rich
Regulars: Reed, Henderson, Davis, McCormick, Plumb, Olsen, Williams, Knight, Lookinland
Guest: Fred Pinkard as .... Mr. Stokey

Bobby scrapes his knee badly on his bike and Alice is ready to provide first aid when Carol rushes in and offers to play nurse. Alice realizes a potential conflict when she sees one, and suggests Bobby have Carol take care of it. So the now sensitive Alice starts to refer everyone to Carol, particularly the male members of the household, who are more used to going to Alice. Carol's thrilled and Alice is pleased her efforts paid off.

Trouble is, now Alice starts to feel a bit extraneous around the Brady house. And Marcia, Jan, and Cindy start to feel neglected. Alice has a talk with Mike and Carol, but can't seem to tell them the truth—she claims she has an ill aunt in Seattle and wants to go be with her.

✿

The title is a new take on an old song, "Annie Doesn't Live Here Anymore," written in 1933 by Joe Young and Johnny Burke, and popularized by Guy Lombardo and his Royal Canadians. It was rerecorded in the '60s by actor Tony Randall, a well-known opera and music buff. When Randall appeared on Johnny Carson's Tonight Show at about this time, he would frequently sing obscure songs from the '20s and '30s, particularly the Lombardo novelty numbers. He recorded two albums of the songs (Warm & Wavery and Vo, Vo, De, Oh, Doe) and reintroduced the nation to Guy Lombardo's brother Carmen, who sang vocals with the band when they first got started and couldn't afford a singer. The albums by Randall triggered a mini-boom in absolutely authentic, full-orchestra recordings of songs from the flapper era and the jazz age, notably by

Britain's Pasadena Roof Orchestra. Incidentally, the film Al-ice Doesn't Live Here Anymore, which won Ellen Burstyn her Oscar and spawned several TV series, wasn't released until 1974.

5. "KATCHOO"
October 24, 1969
Written by William Cowley
Directed by John Rich
Regulars: Reed, Henderson, Davis, McCormick, Plumb, Ol-sen, Williams, Knight, Lookinland

Jan's got the sneezes and Carol thinks she's got a cold. But by the next day, it seems Jan's allergic to something. She doesn't sneeze at all while Mike's out of the house. And she starts sneezing when he gets home. They can't figure it all out. But then they realize she sneezes when Tiger is on the bed. It's definitely the dog.

Mike has a talk with the boys (who've raised Tiger from a pup). They all realize Tiger will have to go—perhaps to their grandparents' house. Greg brings Tiger a good-bye bone, but the dog is so intent on the bone, he ignores the guys' heartfelt farewell speeches.

❀

According to Barry Williams in his book, Growing Up Brady, *Robert Reed nearly quit the show after the fourth or fifth episode. He blamed his discontent on the scripts and John Rich's direction. It wasn't long before the director was changed. Interestingly, Tina Louise had the same reaction to Rich on* Gilligan's Island *and was miserable until Richard Donner directed a couple of episodes and gave her char-acter a new focus. Rich is an excellent director, but actors are famous for liking certain kinds of directors and not oth-ers. It was probably just a case of fitting the right director to a certain actor or acting style.*

6. "A CLUBHOUSE IS NOT A HOME"
October 31, 1969
Written by Skip Webster
Directed by John Rich
Regulars: Reed, Henderson, Davis, McCormick, Plumb, Olsen, Williams, Knight, Lookinland

The family is unpacking all the cartons that have arrived from storage. Closet space is at a premium and the boys are getting a little irritated as the girls boss them around while they are bringing up the cartons. The guys go on strike and retreat to their backyard clubhouse. Mike finds them there and Bobby, Greg, and Peter agree to be more cooperative, but it isn't five minutes before Greg and Marcia are fighting over bathroom counter space, Jan has stolen the "Private, Keep Out" sign from the boys' clubhouse for her bedroom door, and Cindy and Bobby battle over an Indian headband and buckskin jacket.

Mike lays down the law and all is well until the girls invade the boys' clubhouse, installing curtains and dolls. Mike takes such a firm stand about the clubhouse being a male sanctuary, he reduces Cindy to tears. The entire house turns into an armed camp.

✿

Barry Williams notes that Lloyd Schwartz insisted that anything on the show that was supposed to be built by the kids really be built by the kids, and the clubhouse was. It's a wonder the notoriously strong studio craft unions didn't object.

7. "KITTY KARRY-ALL IS MISSING"
November 11, 1969
Written by Al Schwartz and Bill Freedman
Directed by John Rich
Regulars: Reed, Henderson, Davis, McCormick, Plumb, Olsen, Williams, Knight, Lookinland
Guest: Pitt Herbert as..........................Mr. Driscoll

Cindy's playing with her doll, Kitty Karry-All, when Bobby starts giving her a hard time about her affection for it. Cindy leaves the room for a minute, and when she comes back, the doll is gone. Cindy immediately suspects Bobby, but he claims he didn't touch it. The entire family is mobilized and everyone searches the house for hours. The rest of the kids ostracize Bobby until Mike has a talk with them.

The kids have a mock trial with Bobby as the defendant, but the jury (Jan and Peter) is hung. The family is divided and the problem seems insoluble until Bobby's kazoo turns up missing and the family starts to suspect another culprit is at large.

❧

Kitty Karry-All was a doll manufactured by Remco in 1969, and so-named because she wore a pinafore with numerous pockets that could hold a comb and other necessities. The doll was released in a box with Brady Bunch *graphics, and a photo of Susan Olsen (as Cindy) on it. The doll was not a big seller, and today it's one of the rarest and most desirable* Brady Bunch *collectibles, commanding a price of several hundred dollars.*

8. "A-CAMPING WE WILL GO"
November 14, 1969
Written by Herbert Finn and Alan Dinehart
Directed by Oscar Rudolph
Regulars: Reed, Henderson, Davis, McCormick, Plumb, Olsen, Williams, Knight, Lookinland

The Bradys are going camping and Marcia, Jan, and Cindy are rebelling. They've never been camping, and they don't ever want to go camping. Camping is for boys, or as Cindy says, "Yuck." Carol lays down the law, and Alice treats the whole thing like a military maneuver.

Mike even insists the girls go fishing with them. After hours, Mike and the kids return with one small fish. Cindy screamed and scared all the fish away, Marcia thought Peter's line was a cobweb, and Mike caught Cindy, who fell in.

✿

Alice wearing curlers on a camping trip wasn't all that strange. Nearly everybody wore curlers at the time (except most women on TV), unless they had their hair done every week and teased and sprayed until it was so stiff it didn't move for a week. There were no blow-dryers then, the bonnet-type dryers required immobility for an hour or more, and salon-style dryers were extremely expensive and took up lots of space.

9. "SORRY, RIGHT NUMBER"
November 21, 1969
Written by Ruth Brooks Flippen
Directed by George Cahan
Regulars: Reed, Henderson, Davis, McCormick, Plumb, Olsen, Williams, Knight, Lookinland
Guests: Allan Melvin as.............................Sam
         Howard Culver as.................. Mr. Crawford

The Brady household is desperately in need of more phone lines. Mike gets his own line in his den (the kids have another one in the family room). But before Mike knows it, Greg's in the den using his phone because Carol's on the other one. Mike goes back into the den and finds Peter on his phone. He issues an ultimatum that the kids can't use his phone.

But the kids start fighting over the other phone and Carol presents them with an egg timer, limiting their calls. When the phone bill comes, Mike freaks. He's determined to teach the kids the value of money. So, he installs a pay phone.

✿

The title brings to mind the 1948 classic film, Sorry, Wrong Number, directed by Anatole Litvak, and starring Barbara Stanwyck, Burt Lancaster, and William Conrad. It was based on a famous radio thriller, and was remade as a cable movie in 1989 with Loni Anderson.

Allan Melvin

Allan Melvin, who plays Alice's ever-lovin' Sam the Butcher, had his first TV successes in uniform, playing the lively Corporal Henshaw to Phil Silvers's *Sergeant Bilko*, an army pal of Dick Van Dyke's on his show, and Sgt. Hacker in *Gomer Pyle, U.S.M.C.* According to an interview in *The TV Collector* magazine, he got his start by joining a little theater group his friend actor Frank Campanella belonged to, and got into radio thanks to his ability as an impressionist. After his work in radio, he performed stand-up comedy in New York clubs. From there, he got a part on Broadway in *Stalag 17* and was then cast in *Bilko*. After *Brady*, he played Barney Hefner on *All in the Family* for a decade, then continued work in voice-overs, providing the voice for Magilla Gorilla and other characters.

---

10. "EVERY BOY DOES IT ONCE"
December 5, 1969
Written by Lois and Arnold Peyser
Directed by Oscar Rudolph
Regulars: Reed, Henderson, Davis, McCormick, Plumb, Olsen, Williams, Knight, Lookinland
Guests: Michael Lerner as .... Johnny
        [Larry McCormick as .... Announcer]

Bobby and Cindy watch *Cinderella* on TV and he's concerned that Carol will turn into a mean stepmother. His fears are amplified when she asks him to clean out the fireplace, and makes him stand for a fitting for Greg and Peter's hand-me-downs. He even feels worse when Jan, Marcia, and Alice all make fun of him in his oversized hand-me-downs.

Carol's mystified by his behavior until Alice tells her that Bobby mentioned he watched *Cinderella.*

Carol has a solution—buy Bobby a new bicycle, but when she and Mike sneak out, the house is empty except for Bobby and Alice, and he's miffed that not one of them said good-bye. Now he has a solution—he'll run away.

❀

We learn the names of the two daughters of Brady neighbor Mr. Dittmeyer, Nancy and Carla. In the 1995 film, The Brady Bunch Movie, *The Dittmeyers have a boy and a girl, Eric and Missy.*

The announcer on the TV show Cindy and Bobby watch is L.A. newscaster Larry McCormick, who frequently played newscasters and announcers on TV shows. He still reports for station KTLA.

11. "VOTE FOR BRADY"
December 12, 1969
Written by Elroy Schwartz
Directed by David Alexander
Regulars: Reed, Henderson, Davis, McCormick, Plumb, Olsen, Williams, Knight, Lookinland
Guests: Martin Ashe as ....Mr. Dickens
Stephen Liss as ....Rusty
Casey Morgan as............................. Scott

Marcia comes home with good news—she was nominated for president of the student body—and bad news—so was Greg. The first conflict arises over the telephone, as both candidates want to call classmates to encourage them to vote for each of them. Then the other four kids start arguing over who's the best candidate. Carol and Mike decide they must be impartial.

Carol suggests that Marcia spend her $10 campaign allocation on posters, while Mike loans Greg his tape recorder to make tapes to play on the loudspeaker between classes. When Marcia's campaign plans are missing and

Greg's tape is erased, they suspect each other, then blame Carol, Mike, and Alice.

✿

Susan Olsen was the cast member who was least like her on-screen character. She frequently objected to the things Cindy did, which were diametrically opposed to her own behavior. She particularly disliked this episode. "There were times when Cindy's nine years old and she has to write signs, 'Vote for Marcia.' Marcia is her sister, and she cannot spell Marcia's name and she's nine years old. There were lots of silly, stupid things that were supposed to be cute, but I was a little old."

12. "THE VOICE OF CHRISTMAS"
December 19, 1969
Written by John Fenton Murray
Directed by Oscar Rudolph
Regulars: Reed, Henderson, Davis, McCormick, Plumb, Olsen, Williams, Knight, Lookinland
Guests: Hal Smith as .... Santa Claus
        Carl Albert as .... The Little Boy
Song: O Come All Ye Faithful .... Carol Brady

Carol's due to sing a solo at church for Christmas, but all her rehearsing is for naught when she loses her voice. The doctor tells her she has rehearsed so much that she has strained her vocal chords. The only chance she has to sing Christmas morning is if she rests and doesn't talk until then. She's frantic, worrying about her Christmas shopping and preparations. But Mike forces her to take it easy and keep her head over a humidifier.

Alice cooks up her home remedy for laryngitis, composed of camphor, vinegar, tar, pepper, and a bunch of other stuff. It smells disgusting, but she soaks a rag in it and makes Carol wrap it around her neck. Cindy has her own remedy: she begs Santa to give her mom her voice back. She's positive that's all it will take.

✿

Florence Henderson's version of the Christmas song was never commercially released.

The exterior of the department store used in the establishing shot was a store in Santa Monica called Henshey's, which went out of business several years ago. The building was damaged in the 1994 Northridge earthquake, but is being completely restored as part of the trendy Third Street Promenade renovation.

13. "IS THERE A DOCTOR IN THE HOUSE?"
December 26, 1969
Written by Ruth Brooks Flippen
Directed by Oscar Rudolph
Regulars: Reed, Henderson, Davis, McCormick, Plumb, Olsen, Williams, Knight, Lookinland
Guests: Marion Ross as . . . . Dr. Porter
          Herbert Anderson as . . . . .Dr. Cameron

Peter comes home from school with the measles and Carol's barely called the doctor when a "spotted" Jan shows up. The two kids start driving Alice batty. Meanwhile, Mike calls his doctor and is surprised Carol hasn't called him. He asks him to stop by the house. The next crisis is Jan yelling that there's a strange man in her room, and Peter screaming that there's a strange woman in his room. Carol's female doctor and Mike's male doctor are both there. Peter doesn't want a woman doctor and Jan isn't thrilled about having a man look at her.

The other four kids come home, all with the measles. The girls want *their* regular doctor, and so do the boys. Carol and Mike don't know what to do. But it's all immaterial as the kids turn Carol, Mike, and Alice into their personal slaves.

✿

Marion Ross, who plays Dr. Porter, was a regular on a number of TV series, including Life with Father, The Gertrude Berg Show, *and* Mr. Novak. *But a guest-starring role on an episode of* Love, American Style, *was spun off into her most memorable series role, that of Marion Cunningham on* Happy Days. *Ross is also an accomplished stage actress, making many appearances on both the West Coast and on Broadway, including a recent national tour in* Arsenic and Old Lace.

If Herbert Anderson (Dr. Cameron) looks familiar, it's because he played Henry Mitchell, father of Dennis the Menace, *from 1959 to 1963, as well as a lot of bumbling characters in films of the '40s and '50s.*

14. "FATHER OF THE YEAR"
January 2, 1970
Written by Skip Webster
Directed by George Cahan
Regulars: Reed, Henderson, Davis, McCormick, Plumb, Olsen, Williams, Knight, Lookinland
Guests: Oliver McGowan as .... Hamilton Samuels
        Bill Mullikin as .... Lance Pierce
        Lee Corrigan as .... Cameraman
        Bob Golden as. .... Mr. Fields

Mike leaves the house late for an important meeting because he's helped Marcia with her math homework. So, when Marcia sees a "Father of the Year" essay contest, she decides to enter Mike. When working on the essay in Mike's den, she's caught by Cindy, Jan, and Mike. Startled, she doesn't screw the top back onto a bottle of white-out, which spills and ruins a set of Mike's blueprints and his notes for a speech.

Mike gives her a list of chores as punishment, but when he comes home the next night, she hasn't done them because she was working on the essay. Mike grounds her for a week.

15. "54–40 AND FIGHT"
January 9, 1970
Written by Burt Styler
Directed by Oscar Rudolph
Regulars: Reed, Henderson, Davis, McCormick, Plumb, Olsen, Williams, Knight, Lookinland
Guest: Herb Vigran as .... Harry

The kids have a hoard of trading stamps—the girls want to redeem them for a sewing machine, while the boys want a rowboat. Each half of the family has saved stamps independently, but now who is going get the treasure trove of stamps Alice has in a kitchen drawer? Mike gives the kids an obvious answer—split them up.

But neither group has enough to get the item they want. So Carol suggests they merge their books of stamps and get one item they can all use. But the kids can't find an item they agree on. They turn the decision back to Carol. She picks a grandfather clock and Mike thinks that's a lousy idea. He wants a pool table. They decide to wait.

Then there's an announcement in the paper that Checker Trading Stamps are going out of business and they will only redeem stamps for 30 days.

✿

There have been bizarre true stories about divorce disputes over custody of season baseball or symphony tickets, so it's not surprising that the newly blended Bradys argue over their "Checker" trading stamps. Trading stamps had been a big part of American life in the '60s. For many years, there were S&H Green Stamps nationwide and Top Value and Plaid Stamps in some regions of the country. In the early 1960s, Blue Chip Stamps burst onto the national market, giving Green Stamps real competition for the first time. Green Stamps were given to only one of each type of merchant in a neighborhood, which could be a definite marketing tool. If you needed gas, the theory was that you'd go to the station giving stamps. But Blue Chip Stamps let anyone anywhere give out its stamps (you got one stamp for each 10 cents in goods purchased). A big stamp war en-

sued, not just between the two competitors, but among Blue Chip Stamp-dispensing merchants. One drug chain would offer double stamps, and another would counter with triple stamps. This was particularly true with gasoline stations, which were quite often located together at intersections, with as many as three or four gasoline stations per intersection, each trying to out-give the other in premiums.

The Hatfields and the McCoys are the famous feuding families who fought and killed each other for decades in the 1800s in West Virginia and Kentucky.

The title of the episode refers to "54–40 or Fight!," the slogan of the Democratic Party under President James K. Polk after his election in 1844. After the War of 1812, the "northwestern boundary dispute" arose and was a burning issue for an entire generation of Americans, nearly leading to another war with England. American expansionists opposed an 1818 treaty which allowed both British and American settlements in the Oregon Territory. A large number of American settlers moved into the area in the ensuing years and demanded the British be pushed back to the 54th parallel (the actual boundary being 54° 40 N). A compromise treaty was signed in 1846, which established the boundary between the U.S. and Canada as we know it today.

16. "MIKE'S HORROR-SCOPE"
January 16, 1970
Written by Ruth Brooks Flippen
Directed by Oscar Rudolph
Regulars: Reed, Henderson, Davis, McCormick, Plumb, Olsen, Williams, Knight, Lookinland
Guests: Abbe Lane as........................Beebe Gallini
         Joe Ross as ....Duane Cartwright [uncredited]

Carol reads her horoscope, which says she shouldn't buy anything tomorrow. Mike's says a "strange woman" will come into his life. The next day, a stunning new client appears in Mike's office. She hires Mike to design a new factory for her cosmetics company. A pink factory.

Beebe Gallini proves to be a demanding client, too, as she ruins Mike's plans to take the boys fishing and Carol has to go in his place. Carol has a horrible day, getting seasick and falling into a pile of fish. Mike's day wasn't much better. He's working very long hours since Ms. Gallini wants her factory to be shaped like a powder puff and to be "fluffy."

❀

The building used as Beebe's current factory in the establishing shot is the old Beverly Hills Public Library. Note that the subtly colored mosaic on the front of the building actually forms a row of books. The library was demolished to make way for a new civic center. This same establishing shot was used for Mike Brady's office for the remaining years of the series. Abbe Lane was the first wife of bandleader Xavier Cugat, one of the musical and comic staples of many films of the '30s and '40s. Despite her use of a variety of accents over the years (including a Gabor-like Hungarian one in this show), Ms. Lane was born in Brooklyn.

17. "THE UNDERGRADUATE"
January 23, 1970
Written by David P. Harmon
Directed by Oscar Rudolph
Regulars: Reed, Henderson, Davis, McCormick, Plumb, Olsen, Williams, Knight, Lookinland
Guests: Gigi Perreau as...............Miss [Linda] O'Hara
Wes Parker as............................. Himself
Teresa Warder as ....Linda [uncredited]

Greg's acting strangely and it isn't just the fact that he flunked a math test. He asks Marcia what girls look for in an "older" man, and she tells him moustaches are really in. Then Alice finds a love note from Greg to a girl named

Linda, replete with quotes from Shakespeare and William Burns. But they're surprised to learn there's no Linda in Greg's math class. What Mike and Carol don't know is that Greg's young, pretty teacher's name is Linda O'Hara.

✿

Gigi Perreau, who plays Greg's math teacher, was a child actress who didn't easily make the transition to adult roles, despite her looks. She was a regular on several TV shows, among them The Betty Hutton Show *and* Follow the Sun. *She also appeared in films, including* Girls Town, Never a Dull Moment, The Man in the Gray Flannel Suit, *and* Dance with Me Henry.

18. "TIGER! TIGER!"
January 30, 1970
Written by Elroy Schwartz
Directed by Herb Wallerstein
Regulars: Reed, Henderson, Davis, McCormick, Plumb, Olsen, Williams, Knight, Lookinland
Guests: Maggie Malooly as.................. Mrs. Simpson
          Gary Grimes as ....Teenage Boy

Tiger disappears one afternoon and he still hasn't returned by the next morning. Mike cancels a golf game and takes Bobby out to look for the dog, but they have no luck. They compose an ad for the paper including a reward of $42.76 (Mike's $25 plus contributions from the rest of the family).

Alice hears there have been several robberies in the neighborhood lately, and she thinks the thieves might have lured Tiger away in order to hit their house. Greg and Peter overhear her telling this to Mike and Carol and they make their own preparations in case the thief strikes tonight. They rig booby traps out of cans and string and hang them over all the doors. Carol hears them and thinks there's something wrong. Mike goes to check that all the doors are locked. Alice does the same thing. Peter and Greg see Alice's shadow and get their baseball bat.

✿

The title brings to mind the film Tora! Tora! Tora!, *which was the battle cry of the Japanese who attacked Pearl Harbor. Tora means Tiger.*

The original Tiger was killed by a car in the beginning of the first season, but this script was already written so the producers got a look-alike dog for the few scenes in which he was needed.

19. "THE BIG SPRAIN"
February 6, 1970
Written by Tam Spiva
Directed by Russ Mayberry
Regulars: Reed, Henderson, Davis, McCormick, Plumb, Olsen, Williams, Knight, Lookinland
Guest: Allan Melvin as .... Sam

Carol is called to the bedside of her sick aunt Mary, and Mike worries running the house will be too much for Alice. She slips on a game of Chinese checkers the kids accidentally leave on the floor and sprains her ankle. Poor Alice will now miss the annual meatcutters' ball on Saturday night. Mike holds a family meeting to see who's going to do the cooking and cleaning—he tells the kids they will.

The next morning the girls are creating such a mess in the kitchen that the boys refuse to set foot in the place. Marcia's screaming that she has to do everything and Jan's yelling because the boys were supposed to wash the dishes, but they refuse to wash dishes if they don't eat. The dismal breakfast defeats Mike's appetite.

The first day's housework is just as bad. The sprinklers flood the backyard, the laundry floats away when Jan puts too much soap in the washing machine, and there are suds all over the dining room.

✿

Note the laundry area outside the door of Alice's room. A few episodes later in "To Move or Not to Move," there is only an empty hallway.

20. "BRACE YOURSELF"
February 13, 1970
Written by Brad Radnitz
Directed by Oscar Rudolph
Regulars: Reed, Henderson, Davis, McCormick, Plumb, Olsen, Williams, Knight, Lookinland
Guests: Molly Dodd as ....Saleslady
Mike Robertson as ....Craig [see below]
John Daniels as ....Eddie
Brian Nash as................................. Joey
Jerry Levreau as .... Harold

Poor Marcia gets braces and thinks she's *ugly, ugly, ugly.*
Marcia's so miserable that she avoids the family, has trouble
eating, and doesn't want to go to school. The kids all try to
compliment her and make her feel less ugly, but nothing
helps. Mike tells her Cleopatra wore braces when she was
a girl, and cheers her up a bit.

How can she go to the school dance? Even with a terrific
new dress? When her date, Alan Anthony, cancels at the
last minute, she's sure the hardware's the reason, though he
insists it's because he has to go out of town with his parents.

❀

*The end credits are incorrect, since there is no character
named Craig in this episode. Mike Robertson plays Alan
Anthony, Marcia's suitor. The actor now goes by the name
of Scott Robertson, and he has a site on the Internet.*

*Note the hangers with faces on them in the dress shop.
These were very popular at the time, and they were also
used in Rhoda's apartment on* The Mary Tyler Moore Show,
which premiered on CBS in 1970, just a year after The
Brady Bunch.

21. "THE HERO"
February 20, 1970
Written by Elroy Schwartz
Directed by Oscar Rudolph

Regulars: Reed, Henderson, Davis, McCormick, Plumb, Olsen, Williams, Knight, Lookinland

Guests: Pitt Herbert as ....Mr. Driscoll
Dani Nolan as ....Mrs. Spencer
Dave Morick as ....Earl Hopkins
Joe Conley as ....Deliveryman
Randy Lane as ....Steve
Iler Rasmussen as ....Jason
Susan Joyce as .... Jennifer
Melanie Baker as ....Tina Spencer

Peter is at a toy store and saves a little girl named Tina Spencer when a large shelving unit nearly falls on her. The proprietor vows to report Peter's bravery to the media. [Today, Mrs. Spencer would immediately go see her lawyer!] Sure enough, a reporter and a photographer from *The Daily Chronicle* show up to do a story about Peter.

Peter's pretty puffed up about the whole thing and soon the rest of the kids are tired of hearing Peter brag. Mrs. Spencer calls Peter down to Driscoll's toy store so she can buy him a present. Lots of presents. Anything he wants. He makes a haul of several dozen things. Carol and Mike see them and tell Peter he's got to return all the gifts except one.

✿

Pitt Herbert, who plays toy shop owner Mr. Driscoll, returned in that role several times during the run of the series (not surprising in a show with six kids). He also appeared several times on Family Affair, The Dick Van Dyke Show, My Three Sons, Nanny and the Professor *and* Wendy and Me.

22. "THE POSSIBLE DREAM"
February 27, 1970
Written by Al Schwartz and Bill Freedman
Directed by Oscar Rudolph
Regulars: Reed, Henderson, Davis, McCormick, Plumb, Olsen, Williams, Knight, Lookinland

Guests: Desi Arnaz, Jr............................ [as himself]
Gordon Jump as............................. Collins
Jonathan Hole as........................Thackery
Pat Patterson as ....Collection Man

Marcia confesses in her diary that she's in love with teen heartthrob Desi Arnaz, Jr. She hides the diary in an old box in the garage. Meanwhile, Carol gives away several boxes of books to the Friend in Need Society. When Cindy's ball rolls into the garage, she finds the diary and adds it to the charity box. Later, Marcia discovers it's missing and is really upset. She's sure someone's taken it, and has read her most secret thoughts.

Jan insists she doesn't have the diary. When Marcia describes it, Cindy tells her what she did. At Alice's suggestion, Mike goes to the Friend in Need office to find the diary and is told the society distributes all books it gets to a variety of used bookstores. A *wide* variety of stores. Meanwhile, Marcia isn't talking to Cindy and puts "No Trespassing" signs on her belongings.

❀

The title brings to mind "The Impossible Dream," the hit song from the 1965 Broadway musical Man of La Mancha. *The star of the show, Richard Kiley, introduced the Mitch Leigh–Joe Darion song, which was then recorded by many other major male pop stars such as Jack Jones, Andy Williams, and Tony Bennett.*

During this period, Desi Arnaz, Jr., appeared on his mother's program, The Lucy Show. *It was filmed at Desilu, which was in another section of the Paramount lot. So he was handy, in addition to being a bona fide teen heartthrob at the time.*

23. "TO MOVE OR NOT TO MOVE"
March 6, 1970
Written by Paul West
Directed by Oscar Rudolph

Regulars: Reed, Henderson, Davis, McCormick, Plumb, Olsen, Williams, Knight, Lookinland
Guests: Fran Ryan as .... Mrs. Hunsaker
Lindsay Workman as.......... Bertram Grossman

The Bradys are busting the seams of their house. The problem's especially critical regarding the kids' bathroom. Carol and Mike have thought about this before but haven't found another house they like as much. But one they do like has come on the market and Mike makes an offer. Suddenly the kids like things the way they are. So does Alice. But they list the house for sale anyway.

Then the family starts hearing strange sounds. To make things worse, they're happening during a week when Mike's got meetings downtown nearly every night.

❀

The title brings to mind the soliloquy from William Shakespeare's Hamlet. *The troubled prince wanders the battlements of his castle saying, "To be or not to be, that is the question."*

When Carol suggests the banging in the night is the wind against the shutters, Alice agrees it might be "If we had shutters." The Brady home does, in fact, have shutters. Mike climbs a ladder to fix one in episode #36, "What Goes Up."

Fran Ryan, who plays Mrs. Hunsaker, the potential buyer of the Bradys' house, was a regular on Gunsmoke, Green Acres, The Doris Day Show, *and* The Wizard.

24. "THE GRASS IS ALWAYS GREENER"
March 13, 1970
Written by David P. Harmon
Directed by George Cahan
Regulars: Reed, Henderson, Davis, McCormick, Plumb, Olsen, Williams, Knight, Lookinland

Baseball practice takes its physical toll on the Brady men, but when Mike complains to Carol, she mentions the problems she has controlling the three girls. Each parent thinks they have the tougher task, and Alice suggests a way to test it: Mike and Carol should switch jobs next Saturday.

Carol bones up on the rules of baseball so she can help the boys with bunting practice, while Mike delves into cookbooks to help Marcia with her scouting cooking badge, while keeping Cindy and Jan out of trouble. The results are pretty dismal, but both of them talk a good game. Carol admits to Alice that Mike was right—his job is harder.

Meanwhile, Mike takes over the kitchen, refusing all advice from Alice. First, he drops a dozen eggs on the floor [note the lovely avocado paper towels], next he tackles the electric mixer and sprays chocolate all over the kitchen, then he breaks every bowl and dirties every pot in the place.

❧

When Alice talks about the great baseball combination, Tinker to Evers to Chance, she refers to three legendary players—Joe Tinker, Johnny Evers, and Frank Chance, stars of the Chicago Cubs early in this century. The three players formed the nucleus of a great team (some sources say the greatest team ever). The Cubbies were 530–235 between 1906 and 1920, a record unequaled to the present. The double plays from shortstop Tinker to Evers at second base to Chance at first base were immortalized in a 1908 poem by Franklin P. Adams in the New York World *entitled "Baseball's Sad Lexicon":*

These are the saddest of possible words:
"Tinker to Evers to Chance."
Trio of bear cubs, and fleeter than birds,
Tinker and Evers and Chance.
Ruthlessly pricking our gonfalon bubble,
Making a Giant hit into a double—
Words that are heavy with nothing but trouble:
"Tinker to Evers to Chance."

Though of course the title is an old axiom, it was current at the time because of Petula Clark's popular song, "The Other Man's Grass Is Always Greener."

25. "LOST LOCKET, FOUND LOCKET"
March 20, 1970
Written by Charles Hoffman
Directed by Norman Abbott
Regulars: Reed, Henderson, Davis, McCormick, Plumb, Olsen, Williams, Knight, Lookinland
Guests: Jack Griffin as .... The Guard

Jan gets a mystery package in the mail—it's a lovely gold heart-shaped locket. She has no idea who sent it. The boys try to find a clue on the package, and spot a dropped "Y" on the typed address label. Carol thinks it's from her aunt Martha, who's the forgetful type. She didn't send it, but they will be getting a totem pole in the mail.

Carol thinks Mike might have sent it and she and Alice sneak down to his office one night to test the typewriter there. But it isn't the suspect machine. They're caught by the security guard, who's suspicious because of a rash of typewriter thefts in the building. But they convince him they're legit. Meanwhile, Mike checks Carol's portable typewriter, but it doesn't have a dropped "Y" either.

That night, Jan wakes up screaming. Her locket is gone from around her neck.

❧

Note that the package is addressed to Jan at their address and "City." This was a common way to address mail sent within your own city—before there were such things as Zip Codes. There were two-digit postal zones in large cities, but you could still address a letter that way in smaller towns.

We learn that Carol Brady has a sister (whose husband's name is Roger) as well as an aunt Martha. Alice also talks about her sisters Emily and Myrtle.

THE SECOND SEASON

1970–1971

FRIDAY NIGHTS—FALL 1970

	ABC	CBS	NBC
7:30	THE BRADY BUNCH	The Interns	The High Chaparral
8:00	Nanny and the Professor		
8:30	The Partridge Family	The Headmaster	The Name of the Game
9:00	That Girl	CBS Friday Night Movie	
9:30	Love, American Style		
10:00	This Is Tom Jones		Bracken's World
10:30			

SEASON RATINGS
October 1970–April 1971

1.	Marcus Welby, M.D.	29.6
2.	The Flip Wilson Show	27.9
3.	Here's Lucy	26.1
4.	Ironside	25.7
5.	Gunsmoke	25.5
6.	ABC Movie of the Week	25.1
7.	Hawaii Five-O	25.0
8.	Medical Center	24.5
9.	Bonanza	23.9
10.	The F.B.I.	23.0
11.	The Mod Squad	22.7
12.	Adam 12	22.6
13.	Rowan & Martin's Laugh-In	22.4
	The Wonderful World of Disney	22.4
15.	Mayberry R.F.D.	22.3
16.	Hee Haw	21.4
17.	Mannix	21.3
18.	The Men from Shiloh	21.2
19.	My Three Sons	20.8
20.	The Doris Day Show	20.7
21.	The Smith Family	20.6
22.	The Mary Tyler Moore Show	20.3
23.	NBC Saturday Night Movie	20.1
24.	The Dean Martin Show	20.0
25.	The Carol Burnett Show	19.8
	The Partridge Family	19.8
	NBC Monday Night Movie	19.8

THE WORLD
1970

- The Chicago Conspiracy Trial concluded with acquittal for the eight defendants who'd been charged with conspiracy to incite the riots at the 1968 Democratic Convention in Chicago. The defendants, leaders of the most visible protest movements of the '60s, included Abbie Hoffman, Jerry Rubin, and Tom Hayden (later to become Jane Fonda's husband and eventually a presidential candidate). They were representatives of the civil disobedience of the prior decade, and the government very much wanted to make examples of them. Five were convicted, though, of crossing state lines to incite a riot.
- Twenty-seven-year-old rocker Jimi Hendrix died. Sixteen days later, the rock world suffered the loss of Janis Joplin.
- Despite the release of their fourth film, *Let It Be*, the Beatles were no more. The group split up and each former member of the Fab Four was performing on his own.
- U.S. airlines introduced the new jumbo jet, the Boeing 747, to the world's skies. In August, the first 747 to be hijacked landed in Cuba.
- France's former president, Charles de Gaulle, died, ending his 30-year dominance of French politics.
- Hemingway's *Islands in the Stream* was considered the most important novel of 1970. Other notable work included Michael Crichton's *Five Patients* and Larry

38

McMurtry's *Moving On*. In nonfiction, corporate America was the target in Robert Townsend's *Up the Organization*.

- Charles Manson and his three disciples went on trial for their lives in a Los Angeles courtroom. Manson was accused of directing his followers to brutally slaughter pregnant actress Sharon Tate and her friends and family in a gruesome night of killing at her rented Bel Air home.

- 1970 was the 75th anniversary of motion pictures (the Lumière Brothers sold tickets to the first motion picture show on December 28, 1895) and there were many festivals commemorating this milestone around the world.

- Abdul Nasser, president of the United Arab Republic, died of a heart attack following an Arab summit meeting.

- The Nobel Prize in Literature was awarded to Russian political novelist Aleksandr I. Solzhenitsyn.

- The films of 1970 reflected the changing social scene. There were more films aimed at young people (*Getting Straight, Woodstock, Medium Cool*) and blacks (*Watermelon Man, Cotton Comes to Harlem*). Once-blacklisted Ring Lardner, Jr., wrote one of the biggest hits of the year, *M*A*S*H*, and other military-themed movies included *Catch-22* and *Patton*. Box office hits included *Butch Cassidy and the Sundance Kid, True Grit*, and Alfred Hitchcock's *Topaz*. The Academy honored *Midnight Cowboy* as best picture and John Schlesinger for best director. John Wayne received the award for Best Actor and Maggie Smith won Best Actress for her performance in *The Prime of Miss Jean Brodie*. Other films of note during the year were *They Shoot Horses, Don't They?; Goodbye, Mr. Chips; Hello, Dolly!; Paint Your Wagon; Five Easy Pieces; Diary of a Mad Housewife*; and *Tora! Tora! Tora!*

- Brooks Robinson led the Baltimore Orioles to victory over the Cincinnati Reds in the fifth game of the World Series.

- Popular music trends included the introduction of reggae, open-air festivals (thanks to the success of Woodstock in 1969), larger bands, and a rise in popularity of albums as opposed to singles. Popular groups of 1970 included Creedence Clearwater Revival; Blood, Sweat and Tears; and Chicago. New artists making their marks included Melanie and the Jackson 5.
- London's *Sunday Times* reported that Jack the Ripper was Edward, Duke of Clarence, a grandson of Queen Victoria.
- It was a lean year on Broadway, with the most notable successes and performances coming from revivals, including Noël Coward's *Private Lives*, with Tammy Grimes and Brian Bedford; Henry Fonda in Thornton Wilder's *Our Town*; and Jimmy Stewart and Helen Hayes in *Harvey*. The big musicals of the year were Stephen Sondheim's blistering commentary on marriage, *Company*, and a musicalized version of *All About Eve*, which was called *Applause*.

TELEVISION
1970

- The Bradys seemed to be the last married couple in America. There were more than a dozen shows on television this year that featured single parents. The shows included *The Doris Day Show, Julia, Here's Lucy, My Three Sons, The Courtship of Eddie's Father, Nanny and the Professor, To Rome with Love, The Partridge*

Family, Mayberry R.F.D., The Governor and J. J., Family Affair and, technically, *Bonanza*. Bill Cosby played surrogate single parent as a bachelor phys. ed. teacher.

- ABC revamped its Monday lineup that fall and premiered *Monday Night Football*.
- CBS proved its commitment to urban reality shows when it broke memorable sitcom ground with *All in the Family*.
- Television had eroded the motion picture audience significantly in most developed countries. At the end of World War II, the British cinema audience numbered 30 million per week. By 1969, weekly attendance had dropped to less than 5 million.
- One of the major events of the year was the premiere of Sir Kenneth Clark's *Civilisation*, a British show that caught on with Americans on educational television.
- There were an estimated 231 million TV sets in use worldwide. Thirty-seven percent of these, or 85 million were in the U.S.
- A 44 percent rate increase from AT&T prompted the three broadcast networks into preparing applications to either launch their own satellites to deliver programming to their affiliates, or to develop their own land-based microwave systems.
- CBS cut the minimum commercial length from 1 minute to 30 seconds.
- Congress banned cigarette advertising on television, effective January 2, 1971.
- Harry Reasoner left NBC for ABC, and Dan Rather was elevated to his first news anchor chair.
- Cable television grew 20 percent during the year, expanding to over 3.7 million homes.
- The aborted moon landing, explosion, and retrieval of the Apollo 13 mission was broadcast by satellite all over the world.
- About $92 million worth of U.S. television programming was exported. The most popular shows were *Bonanza*,

The Carol Burnett Show, Kraft Music Hall, Gunsmoke, and *Perry Mason.*

- New trends in programming addressed the problems of ecology, minority groups and other social issues, including drug abuse.
- *Sesame Street* was the most critically praised children's program of the year. It was broadcast over some 200 noncommercial and commercial stations.
- The FCC (Federal Communications Commission) announced that by the fall of 1971, it would force the networks to turn back one half-hour per night to the local stations. Prime time would now consist of just three hours per night. The FCC originally banned off-network rerun fare from the new "prime-time access" period, but relented when the local stations were unable to produce original programming in time.
- CBS broke with tradition and began to preview its programs to television critics before they aired.
- Chet Huntley retired after 31 years as a news reporter, thus ending one of the most well-known partnerships of TV news. NBC's *The Huntley–Brinkley Report* made "Good night, Chet," "Good night, David" part of the national language.

THE BRADY BUNCH
1970

The Bradys finished their first season with respectable ratings and avid fans, so a second year was assured. The fall 1970 ABC schedule had a solid comedy block, with the Bradys leading off the night, followed by Juliet Mills as a magical housekeeper in *Nanny and the Professor*; a singing Brady-type family—*The Partridge Family*; and Marlo Thomas in *That Girl*. The frothy *Love, American Style* brought up the rear, an amusing show of vignettes and blackout sketches about love that usually involved a large brass bed, and starred lots of familiar faces from TV comedy shows.

The Shirley Jones–David Cassidy–Susan Dey *Partridge Family* made it into the top 25 shows its debut season, but the other Friday night shows weren't far behind.

THE EPISODES

26. "THE DROPOUT"
September 25, 1970
Written by Ben Gershman and Bill Freedman
Directed by Peter Baldwin
Regulars: Reed, Henderson, Davis, McCormick, Plumb, Olsen, Williams, Knight, Lookinland
Guest: Don Drysdale as .... Himself

Mike designs a house for baseball great Don Drysdale. He comes to the Bradys' to approve the final design and Mike wants his sons to meet him. They're thrilled. And when Drysdale admires Greg's pitching, he thinks he's destined for the Cooperstown Hall of Fame.

The next thing they know, Carol and Mike are awakened by the sound of Greg lifting barbells. Then he jogs. He starts memorizing a baseball encyclopedia. Greg's grades start plummeting. When Carol and Mike talk to him, he says his schoolwork doesn't matter. He doesn't care about college; in fact, he's thinking of dropping out of high school. He's going to be a major league star.

✿

Don Drysdale retired from major league baseball in 1969 because of injuries. He played for the Los Angeles Dodgers and had a lifetime mark of 209–106 and, at the time, held the all-time record for consecutive scoreless innings pitched, $58^2/_3$.

27. "THE BABYSITTERS"
October 2, 1970
Written by Bruce Howard
Directed by Oscar Rudolph
Regulars: Reed, Henderson, Davis, McCormick, Plumb, Olsen, Williams, Knight, Lookinland
Guests: Gil Stuart as .... Restaurant Captain
Jerry Jones as .... Police Officer

Mike surprises Carol with dinner reservations and tickets to a sold-out show, but Alice has asked for the night off to help Sam decorate his new apartment. Carol suggests they call a babysitter (Marcia and Greg are humiliated at the very idea). Marcia and Greg suggest they do the babysitting and Carol and Mike agree.

The rest of the kids are a little miffed at the idea of taking orders from their older siblings. Mike runs Greg through an emergency quiz. Then Cindy starts sniffling, but she doesn't have a temperature. The adults finally leave and the kids get fed up real fast with Greg and Marcia's dictatorial ways. The Bradys get to a fancy restaurant and Carol can't concentrate on anything, for worrying. Both of them keep calling home, but the line's endlessly busy.

✿

Barry Williams notes that this episode is one where the audience gets a good sense of the layout of the Brady house.

In his book, he says the rooms in the downstairs portion of the house were connected like a real house. The upstairs rooms were in another section of the soundstage.

28. "THE SLUMBER CAPER"
October 9, 1970
Written by Tam Spiva
Directed by Oscar Rudolph
Regulars: Reed, Henderson, Davis, McCormick, Plumb, Olsen, Williams, Knight, Lookinland
Guests: E. G. Marshall as .... J. P. Randolph
Chris Charney as ....Paula
Hope Sherwood as.................Jenny [Wilton]
Barbara Henderson as ....Ruthie
Carolyn Reed as ....Karen

After much discussion, Carol and Mike agree to let Marcia have a slumber party. Alice is thinking of nailing down the furniture; Mike is thinking he and Carol should spend the night in the garage; the boys are thinking of disappearing, and the girls are thinking of what to serve. When Cindy finds out that everybody at slumber parties mostly talks about boys, she's not so pleased with the idea.

The boys start planning tricks to play on the girls and their guests and they offer to "freshen up" the sleeping bags— with itching powder.

At school the next day, Marcia's penalized for an unflattering drawing of her teacher. She insists the drawing was a copy of a picture of George Washington in her classroom, and someone else added the insulting words and her teacher's name under it. She has to stay after school all week, and Mike and Carol tell her she can't have the slumber party. Marcia's really upset that her parents don't believe her and says she doesn't want the party—or anything from them *ever*.

✿

When Alice says, "The party's over, but the melody lingers on," she's adapting the title of an Irving Berlin song from 1927, "The Song Is Ended (But the Melody Lingers On)."

This episode is nepotism at its finest. Carolyn Reed is Robert Reed's daughter, Barbara Henderson is Florence's daughter, Hope Sherwood belongs to Sherwood Schwartz, and E. G. Marshall was Reed's co-star in the TV series The Defenders. Hope Sherwood enjoyed the experience and returned to the show as a girlfriend of Greg's.

29. "THE UN-UNDERGROUND MOVIE"
October 16, 1970
Written by Albert E. Lewin
Directed by Jack Arnold
Regulars: Reed, Henderson, Davis, McCormick, Plumb, Olsen, Williams, Knight, Lookinland

Greg has an unconventional American history teacher and for an assignment he decides to make a movie about the Pilgrims. He borrows some props from school, including a stock and fort fencing. It becomes quite the family project. Mike, Carol, and Alice all horn in while Greg's writing the screenplay and the girls all fight over who is going to play Priscilla, the heroine. Greg tells Peter he'll play John Alden, while Bobby is Miles Standish, but they both want to play Indians.

Greg cancels the movie because he's getting so much static from everyone. It's his project. Carol and Mike apologize and promise he'll get the other kids' cooperation. Carol and Alice make costumes while the kids build the sets—to Greg's specifications. He casts Jan as Priscilla, and the movie starts to take shape. But when everybody gets tired and wants lunch, Greg has a typical director's fit and it looks like the movie is stalled.

✿

Mike Brady has an 8mm film camera. There were no home video cameras in 1970. Most home movie cameras had no sound and each reel of film ran about three minutes. A good movie camera at the time cost around $200, a roll of film about $10 plus processing. If you wanted to make a film longer than 3 minutes, you had to buy a splicer, splicing tape, and larger reels onto which you rewound the longer film. Just as with 16mm and 35mm movie film, to cut scenes together, you needed a moviola, an expensive proposition. Special effects would require professional editing equipment.

30. "GOING GOING . . . STEADY"
October 23, 1970
Written by David P. Harmon
Directed by Oscar Rudolph
Regulars: Reed, Henderson, Davis, McCormick, Plumb, Olsen, Williams, Knight, Lookinland
Guests: Billy Corcoran as.................. Harvey Klinger
Rory Stevens as .... Lester

Marcia's walking on air. In fact she's in orbit. Carol diagnoses the affliction as puppy love with one Harvey Klinger. Greg thinks he's a grade-A creep. But soon, the bubble bursts and Marcia complains that Harvey doesn't know she's alive. She wants to die.

Carol asks Mike what makes a girl appealing to a 14-year-old boy. Marcia says Harvey likes bugs, so she tries to learn all about them. Marcia goes on the attack and presents Harvey with a particularly juicy specimen. Harvey asks her to go steady.

❀

When Alice compares Marcia's misery to Camille, she's referring to Alexander Dumas's famous heroine, who has been the subject of operas, paintings, books, and movies. The most famous is Greta Garbo's Camille (1937), where she convincingly portrays the tragic woman who gives up her own happiness to prove her love.

31. "CALL ME IRRESPONSIBLE"
October 30, 1970
Written by Bruce Howard
Directed by Hal Cooper
Regulars: Reed, Henderson, Davis, McCormick, Plumb, Olsen, Williams, Knight, Lookinland
Guests: Jack Collins .... Mr. Phillips
Annette Ferra.................... Randy [Peterson]
Barbara Morrison .... Drama Coach
William Benedict .... News Vendor
Gordon Jump........................... Mechanic
Bob Peoples.......................... Mr. Peterson

Greg wants a car. He's willing to get a part-time job after school to pay for it. He's thinking of his future. He wants to get a job that has something to do with his goals. Greg's decided he wants to be an architect like his father, so he'd like a job at Mike's office. Mike arranges it, but Greg's disappointed that it will involve mostly cleaning up the office and making deliveries.

Greg still has the idea he should start at the top—both in the job and with a car. And he's got a girl he's trying to impress with all this. When Mike has an urgent delivery of some original plans for a low-cost housing project, he gives the blueprints to Greg to take to be duplicated. But Greg stops at the newsstand to buy a car magazine and the plans slip out of the tube. When he goes back, they're gone. Mike has to stay up all night duplicating them and Greg is fired.

❀

If you wonder where all that spotless small-town scenery is, all the exterior scenes for this episode were filmed on the Paramount lot. Most studios build each building in a different architectural style so that the lots not only look like cities, but buildings of different styles are available to be used for just this purpose.

Annette Ferra was named after Mouseketeer Annette Funicello, who was a close friend of her older sister Sandy. Annette was a child actress, and performed in several episodes of Lassie. *Her sister Sandy is married to radio great and game show host Wink Martindale.*

32. "THE TREASURE OF SIERRA AVENUE"
November 6, 1970
Written by Gwen Bagni and Paul Dubov
Directed by Oscar Rudolph
Regulars: Reed, Henderson, Davis, McCormick, Plumb, Olsen, Williams, Knight, Lookinland
Guest: Victor Killian as ....: Mr. Stoner

Bobby, Greg, and Peter are playing football in a vacant lot on Sierra Avenue and when Bobby's collecting a long pass, he finds an old wallet packed with money. They take it home and count it, and there's $1,100 in it. They figure out that each of them will get $366.66. Then their "loving sisters" come in and admire the money. They'd like the guys to share it . . . or they won't talk to them. Mike comes home with the solution. He's taking it to the police.

The guys still hope it won't be claimed and they'll get it, but then Greg shows Peter an ad from the classifieds about a lost brown wallet with a large sum of money. It offers a reward and contains a phone number. Peter and Greg wrestle with their consciences over whether to call the person. They do, and it's the wrong wallet. The Brady house turns into an armed camp with everyone sniping at everyone else, and it's the last straw when Mike finds out Greg's pricing cars and Peter's offered to buy a friend's ten-speed bike.

❀

The title brings to mind the 1948 Humphrey Bogart classic film The Treasure of the Sierra Madre, *a story of greed.*

33. "A FISTFUL OF REASONS"
November 13, 1970
Written by Tam Spiva
Directed by Oscar Rudolph
Regulars: Reed, Henderson, Davis, McCormick, Plumb, Olsen, Williams, Knight, Lookinland
Guests: Russell Schulman as .... Buddy Hinton
          Ceil Cabot as..........................Mrs. Hinton
          Paul Sorensen as ....Mr. Hinton

Cindy comes home from school in tears after she's picked on by a classmate who makes fun of her lisp. Everybody in the family tries to help her correct it. Cindy works tirelessly with a tongue-twister book but the older boy still won't let up. Peter tells Buddy to get lost and stop teasing Cindy. But Peter won't fight Buddy. Buddy spreads the word that Peter is chicken.

   Mike suggests "calm, cool reason" is better than violence. That's swell, but nobody told Buddy Hinton, and Peter comes home with a beaut of a shiner. Mike tries to practice what he preaches with Buddy's father, but the bully's father is a bully, too.

✿

   The title brings to mind the 1964 Clint Eastwood western A Fistful of Dollars.

   Note that the Hinton backyard is simply the thinly disguised Brady backyard, Astroturf and all.

34. "THE NOT-SO-UGLY DUCKLING"
November 20, 1970
Written by Paul West
Directed by Irving J. Moore
Regulars: Reed, Henderson, Davis, McCormick, Plumb, Olsen, Williams, Knight, Lookinland
Guests: Joseph Mell as.............................Druggist
          Mark Gruner as ....Clark Tyson

Jan's swooning over a new boy, Clark Tyson, but after he meets Marcia, he forgets Jan exists. She confronts Marcia, who tells Jan it's not her fault if Clark doesn't find her attractive. Jan consults Greg about why boys drop girls, and she thinks it's her "crummy face" that turned off Clark.

Mike and Carol decide that what Jan needs to cheer her up is a surprise birthday party. Meanwhile, Jan tries lemons to lighten her freckles. Then she overhears Peter, who walked home with Clark Tyson and a new girl, Jenny, who is a knockout—with lots of freckles. She finally makes up a new boyfriend, George Glass, to save face in the family. But the other kids wonder why they've never seen or heard of him. Marcia checks and there's no George Glass at school, and Greg checks and there's no boy by that name in the whole city.

✿

"The Ugly Duckling" is one of Hans Christian Andersen's most famous stories, about a plain brown cygnet raised among ducklings who deride the other bird for being ugly and ungainly. The cygnet has the last laugh when it grows into a regal swan.

We learn the Brady's phone number in this episode: 762-0799. About this time, the phone company allocated 555 numbers for its own use. The surplus numbers were available for movies and TV shows to use as non-working numbers. Part of the reason was when an actual phone number was used on a national TV show, people with that number in cities throughout the country would start getting nuisance calls.

35. "THE TATTLETALE"
December 4, 1970
Written by Sam Locke and Milton Pascal
Directed by Russ Mayberry
Regulars: Reed, Henderson, Davis, McCormick, Plumb, Olsen, Williams, Knight, Lookinland
Guest: John Wheeler as .... The Postman

Cindy regales everyone at the breakfast table with stories
about the neighbors; she tattles on Peter, who strained a
guppy from the fish tank with the top of the salt shaker; and
then tattles on Greg. Mike gives her a talking to, but she
keeps it up. Cindy tattles on Bobby and he calls her a fink.
Also adding to the Brady craziness, Tiger's taken to snatch-
ing stuff, and Alice is entering contests.

When the mailman delivers a letter telling Alice she won
a jingle contest, Cindy answers the phone. It's Sam, who's
taking Alice to a dance that night, but Cindy tells him Alice
is hugging the postman. Sam's furious. He tells Cindy *not*
to tell Alice he called. That night, Alice is concerned when
Sam's very late. She calls him, and he tells her to get the
postman to take her to the dance and then hangs up.

✿

*Susan Olsen loathes this episode. "I wasn't that dramat-
ically different [from Cindy]," she says now, "but being
very sensitive and young, I got very sensitive to the things
she had to do that I wouldn't, like tattling on her siblings.
That's something I would never have done."*

*The hi-fi Alice wins cost $98 new. It was a popular
model, as it had detachable speakers hinged on each side
which could be removed and placed elsewhere for opti-
mum stereo listening.*

*Mike brings home a Gilbert and Sullivan record and Mar-
cia jokes about them being a new band. Sir William Gilbert
and Sir Arthur Sullivan were the foremost proponents of
light opera, and reigned supreme in the London theater
from 1875 through 1889 until Sullivan's untimely death.
But their glorious music and biting satirical view of society
live on even today, and their many operettas are still performed in high schools, churches, and even Broadway and
West End theaters. In 1970, the D'Oyly Carte Opera Company was still visiting the U.S. West Coast each summer,
performing at the Pasadena Civic Auditorium and the
San Francisco Opera House each July and August. "A*

Wand'ring Minstrel," the song Mike sings a bit of, is from
Gilbert and Sullivan's most famous work, The Mikado.

36. "WHAT GOES UP"
December 11, 1970
Written by William Raynor and Myles Wilder
Directed by Leslie H. Martinson
Regulars: Reed, Henderson, Davis, McCormick, Plumb, Ol-
　　sen, Williams, Knight, Lookinland
Guests: Jimmy Bracken as .... Jimmy
　　　　Sean Kelly as .... Tim
　　　　Brian Tochi as .... Tommy

Bobby wants to join Peter's treehouse club, but the rest of
the members think he's too young. Peter suggests they make
him their mascot, and send him up for the initiation, but he
falls out of the tree, spraining his ankle. Mike and Carol give
Bobby a parakeet, and he spends his recuperation time
teaching it to talk. Tiger scares it and it's let loose in the
house. When the parakeet flies to Bobby, he's impressed.
　　His ankle's better and Peter and his friends take him to
the treehouse to be initiated, but he can't do it, suffering
from a case of acrophobia. He claims his ankle still hurts
and limps back to the house. Then Jan challenges him to
swing higher than she does, and he doesn't want to do that
either. Or go on a picnic at Mt. Claymore. Pretty soon, he
doesn't want to leave his room.

✿

　　Barry Williams confesses to one of the few big boo-boos
in this episode that made it to the screen. In the backyard
scene when they're trying to interest Bobby in joining them,
Greg turns to Jan and clearly calls her "Eve" when urging
her to try the trampoline.

37. "CONFESSIONS, CONFESSIONS"
December 18, 1970
Written by Brad Radnitz
Directed by Russ Mayberry
Regulars: Reed, Henderson, Davis, McCormick, Plumb, Olsen, Williams, Knight, Lookinland
Guest: Snag Werris as .... Hardware Man

Peter gets ready early for his first overnight camp-out, while Greg and Bobby start shooting free throws into their wastebasket. Though Carol told them not to play ball in the house, Peter's shot goes wide, the ball bounces down the hall, over the stair banister and right into Carol's favorite vase, smashing it into three pieces. Peter's sure he'll be grounded and he'll miss the camping trip. Greg suggests they glue it together and not tell their mom until the weekend's over.

Marcia and Jan find out, but promise not to tell. The boys go to the hardware store to get glue, and run into Carol. She's immediately suspicious, but can't figure out what they're up to. That night, Carol puts cut flowers in the vase and during dinner the vase slowly starts to leak through the crack repairs. Then it springs a number of leaks, spurting water all over the dinner table.

❁

The boys buy white glue to repair the vase, which isn't the right glue. Any hardware man worth his salt at the time would have recommended Duco Cement (there were no super glues at the time).

When Alice sees the leaking vase, she wonders if anyone has "three coins for the fountain," which brings to mind the 1954 hit film, Three Coins in the Fountain. *The ultra-romantic film (starring Louis Jourdan, Rossano Brazzi, and Dorothy McGuire) and its popular title song added the phrase to the language. Alice also says frequently, "Would you believe . . . ," a reference to the popular spy spoof TV comedy* Get Smart.

When Carol suggests they get Bobby to tell the truth by giving him a lantern, she refers to Diogenes, a Greek philosopher who lived 300 years before Christ. He wandered the town in daylight with a lit lantern, seeking an honest man, thus exposing men's selfishness and vanity. He had contempt for the luxuries of life, and lived in a tub. His nickname was "Dog."

38. "THE IMPRACTICAL JOKER"
January 1, 1971
Written by Burt Styler
Directed by Oscar Rudolph
Regulars: Reed, Henderson, Davis, McCormick, Plumb, Olsen, Williams, Knight, Lookinland
Guest: Lennie Bremen........................ Exterminator

Jan nearly gives Alice heart failure by putting a plastic ink spot on Alice's new coat, then nails Marcia with a plastic spider. Carol tells Jan to cool it or her practical jokes are going to get her into trouble.

Later, Greg brings home a white mouse from school for a science project—he has to teach the mouse (Myron) to run a maze over the weekend. Jan borrows the mouse to scare Marcia and Cindy, and Carol says no mouse in the house. Mike gets home and suggests the mouse and the science project reside in the garage. But in the middle of the night, Greg remembers the neighbor's cat and the boys all go out to check on Myron. He's fine, and Greg takes him upstairs. But Jan is watching all this from her window. She sneaks into their room, takes Myron, and hides him in the clothes hamper in the girls' room. During the night, Myron chews through the wicker hamper and escapes.

❧

There are a number of inside stories relating to this episode, which began a period of practical joking among the kids on the show. Also, Robert Reed was particularly critical of this show, feeling it was one of their worst. All the tales, told firsthand, can be found in the book by Barry Williams and Chris Kreski, Growing Up Brady.

39. "WHERE THERE'S SMOKE"
January 8, 1971
Written by David P. Harmon
Directed by Oscar Rudolph
Regulars: Reed, Henderson, Davis, McCormick, Plumb, Olsen, Williams, Knight, Lookinland
Guests: Craig Hundley as .... Tommy [Johnson]
　　　　　Marie Denn as ....Mrs. Johnson
　　　　　Gary Marsh as................................. Phil
　　　　　Bobby Kramer as...........................Johnny
Song: "Till I Met You"........................ Greg Brady

Greg is invited to play the guitar at a gig with some school friends. They all smoke, and Greg thinks he has to as well to fit in. The group, which plays rock, is called The Banana Convention. Cindy and Jan see Greg smoking and debate with Marcia over whether to tell their parents. They do, and Mike and Carol talk to him about it. Mike admits he smoked when he was younger. Greg says it's the first time and he won't do it again.

　　Carol joins a friend, Mrs. Johnson, in an antismoking committee. At a meeting at the Brady house, a pack of cigarettes falls out of Greg's jacket pocket in front of Mrs. Johnson. Greg says they're not his, but Mrs. Johnson doesn't believe him, even if Carol does. Greg just wants to know who put the cigarettes in his pocket.

✿

　　The song in this episode, "Till I Met You," had not been recorded until it was used in 1995's The Brady Bunch Movie, *where it's performed by Christopher Daniel Barnes (who plays Greg) and is available on the movie's soundtrack. It was written by Barry Williams, Lloyd Schwartz, and Sherwood Schwartz.*

40. "WILL THE REAL JAN BRADY PLEASE STAND UP?"
January 15, 1971
Written by Al Schwartz and Bill Freedman
Directed by Peter Baldwin
Regulars: Reed, Henderson, Davis, McCormick, Plumb, Olsen, Williams, Knight, Lookinland
Guests: Pamelyn Ferdin as .... Lucy
Marcia Wallace as .... Saleswoman
Karen Foulkes as .... Margie

Jan's having an identity crisis and she's sick of being an invisible middle kid. She's Marcia's younger sister and Cindy's older sister. She gets inspiration from a magazine photo and buys a black wig. It looks ridiculous on her. Greg says she looks like Davy Crockett, and the guys can't stop laughing. Jan's pretty upset. She tells Carol and Mike she wants to wear it all the time so people will notice her. She begs to wear it to a friend's birthday party. Mike and Carol say it's okay, since it seems to mean so much to her.

Meanwhile, Peter, who's also invited to the party, learns a girl who's been chasing him will be there, and decides to get the flu.

❁

The title is a line used several times a night on a quiz show called To Tell the Truth, *which ran from 1956 to 1967 on CBS. The program was slightly similar to the classic* What's My Line? *except that instead of guessing one person's occupation the celebrity panel was confronted with three contestants, all claiming to be one person. During the questioning, the actual person told the truth and the other two lied. At the end of the game, Bud Collyer said, "Will the real* (whoever) *please stand up?"*

The department store used in the establishing shot when Jan goes shopping is the old May Co. at La Brea and Fairfax, in the Mid-Wilshire district near the La Brea Tar Pits and the Los Angeles County Museum. Due to a series of department store mergers and development plans, the store was closed in 1994.

Marcia Wallace went on to play the receptionist Carol Kester Bondurant on The Bob Newhart Show from 1972 to 1978.

41. "THE DRUMMER BOY"
January 22, 1971
Written by Tom and Helen August
Directed by Oscar Rudolph
Regulars: Reed, Henderson, Davis, McCormick, Plumb, Olsen, Williams, Knight, Lookinland
Guests: David "Deacon" Jones as .... Himself
Bart La Rue as .... Coach
Jimmy Bracken as .... Larry
Dennis McDougall as .... Freddy
Pierre Williams as .... Jimmy

Peter, Cindy, and Jan get into the glee club and Bobby's depressed that he didn't make it (he can't carry a tune). Carol suggests he might be interested in learning a musical instrument. Guess which instrument he chooses? The drums. Oh, joy. Soon, the noise is unbearable.

Meanwhile, Peter's really an overachiever. He's also offensive end on the football team and Rams great Deacon Jones is helping coach them. But his teammates tease him unmercifully about his participation in the glee club.

Bobby's progress on the drums isn't so hot (but it's loud). Mike comes up with the perfect solution, and sets up a studio for Bobby in the garage. Peter tells Carol and Mike he's going to quit the glee club because his football team members think singing is sissy. Then the neighbors call to complain about Bobby's drumming.

❀

Ah, for the good old days when Los Angeles had a professional football team. And a defensive end as good as David "Deacon" Jones.

When Mike says "The beat, beat of the tom-toms" is clogging up his head, he's quoting a line from Cole Porter's "Night and Day." Porter said the rhythm came from a Mohammedan calling the faithful to worship in Morocco. It was published in 1932 and was written for Porter's show The Gay Divorce *(which became the Fred Astaire–Ginger Rogers musical film* The Gay Divorcee*). The ludicrous film biography of Porter's life,* Night and Day *(1946, starring Cary Grant and Alexis Smith), created a wholly fictional story about the writing of this, Porter's most famous song.*

42. "COMING OUT PARTY"
January 29, 1971
Written by David P. Harmon
Directed by Oscar Rudolph
Regulars: Reed, Henderson, Davis, McCormick, Plumb, Olsen, Williams, Knight, Lookinland
Guests: John Howard as . . . . Dr. Howard
           Jack Collins as . . . . Mr. Phillips

Mike's boss, Mr. Phillips, invites the whole Brady clan to go deep-sea fishing on his boat. Most of the kids have other plans but agree to change them. Carol warns them all to stay healthy, but the words are barely out of her mouth when Cindy sneezes. Mike gives them all lessons with the old rod and reel. But Cindy gets sicker and Dr. Howard diagnoses tonsillitis, and schedules their removal for Saturday. Cindy would rather go fishing. So would Greg and Peter, who are down in the dumps about missing the trip. But Mike reschedules it for a week later.

When Dr. Howard returns to check Cindy, she refuses to let him look at her throat, so Carol demonstrates. He says Carol's tonsils are as bad as Cindy's. He orders them both to the hospital immediately. After the operations, they're both in bed with orders not to talk. After Mike's orders not to answer the phone, Carol does and insults his boss (and his boat), thinking it's Mike testing her. Mike tries to apologize, but Mr. Phillips hangs up on him.

❀

Today the phrase "coming out party" might have several meanings. Though used as a joke here, in 1971 the phrase meant a debutante party, where a young woman in a certain level of society, who was 18 or older, was "presented" to society. The event signaled a round of parties, where eligible young men were introduced to the young women. In earlier times, the event also was the point where a young woman could bare her shoulders in public, dress in high heels, and wear her hair up.

When Alice says, "Go down to the sea again . . . in ships," she quotes from the Bible (Psalms 107:23): "They that go down to the sea in ships, that do business in great waters."

When Mike gives the family fishing lessons, he teaches them fly casting, more appropriate to lake fishing than to a deep-sea fishing expedition.

43. "OUR SON, THE MAN"
February 5, 1971
Written by Albert E. Lewin
Directed by Jack Arnold
Regulars: Reed, Henderson, Davis, McCormick, Plumb, Olsen, Williams, Knight, Lookinland
Guests: Julie Cobb as . . . . The Girl
         Chris Beaumont as . . . . The Boy

Greg's really bugged by his lack of privacy. He thinks he deserves more around the house, now that he's a "man" in high school. He wants his own room. Mike and Carol discuss converting the garage, giving Greg Mike's den, or the family room. Mike gives in to guilt and gives Greg his den.

Greg turns it into a psychedelic pad. What's next, women? Yep.

❀

The title brings to mind the comedy records of Allan Sherman, the first of which was titled, "My Son, the Folksinger," which was itself a joke as Sherman was heavy, balding, and Jewish. He did parodies of common old time folk and classical songs with very contemporary lyrics. The album was a huge hit (particularly the kid's letter from camp, "Hello Muddah, Hello Faddah, Here I am at Camp Granada"), and engendered any number of "My Son, the———" jokes, books, and the like.

44. "THE LIBERATION OF MARCIA BRADY"
February 12, 1971
Written by Charles Hoffman
Directed by Russ Mayberry
Regulars: Reed, Henderson, Davis, McCormick, Plumb, Olsen, Williams, Knight, Lookinland
Guests: John Lawrence as .... The Man
Ken Sansom as .... Stan Jacobsen
Ken Jones as............................ Interviewer
Claire Wilcox as .... Judy Winters

A reporter comes to Marcia's campus to interview some of the young women about how they feel about women's liberation. He doesn't get much response until he talks to Marcia. She says she thinks girls are the equal of boys, and as for whether she can do anything her brothers can, she says she'd at least like the opportunity to try. But as soon as she's spoken, she's afraid she's made a mistake. What are the men in the family going to think when they see her on the news?

But that's the whole point, isn't it? She should be able to speak out if she wants. But as the news is about to begin, she pretends the TV is broken. Of course, the whole family watches and Greg ridicules her as soon as it's over. Marcia says she meant what she said and pretty soon the whole house is divided along gender lines.

Marcia tries to think of how to prove she can do anything a boy can, and comes up with a great idea. She'll join Greg's Frontier Scout troop. The guys retaliate by making Peter join Marcia's club, the Sunflower Girls.

❀

The title brings to mind the 1970 film, The Liberation of L. B. Jones, *famed director William Wyler's last film. It stars Lee J. Cobb, Anthony Zerbe, and Roscoe Lee Browne, and concerns racism in the south.*

When the astonished man Peter tries to sell Sunshine Girl cookies to asks if they're on a "hidden camera" show, he refers to the long-running Candid Camera. *The show ran from 1948 to 1953 on NBC and from 1960 to 1967 on CBS, and it used to put people in situations just like this one.*

Claire Wilcox, who plays Judy Winters, was a child star who appeared in the 1963 film Forty Pounds of Trouble *with Tony Curtis. Ken Jones, the news reporter in the episode, was a real southern California newscaster at the time.*

45. "LIGHTS OUT"
February 19, 1971
Written by Bruce Howard
Directed by Oscar Rudolph
Regulars: Reed, Henderson, Davis, McCormick, Plumb, Olsen, Williams, Knight, Lookinland
Guests: Snag Werris as .... Store Owner
Lindsay Workman as............... Schoolteacher
Joseph Tatner as...........................Warren

All of a sudden, Cindy's afraid to sleep with the lights off. When Marcia and Jan object, Cindy begs to sleep with Carol and Mike. They find out that she was frightened by a trick a magician did at a friend's party. He made a lady disappear and Cindy ran out and never saw the lady again.

Peter decides to try out for a school vaudeville show as a magician. Mike takes Peter to a magic shop, where they buy the linking rings and jumping bottle tricks and the blueprints for a disappearing cabinet (like the one the magician who scared Cindy used). Mike builds the cabinet and Peter trains Cindy to be his assistant. But Cindy refuses to get in the cabinet.

❀

The exterior of the school used in the establishing shot is a small grassy square on the Gower Street side of the Paramount Studios lot. That side of the property was once RKO Studios, then Desilu, then it became part of the adjoining larger studio, Paramount. This little square, which has studio offices on three sides and a street and soundstage on the fourth, has been used endless times in TV shows and films. For many years, Gene Roddenberry (Star Trek) had his office on the square (to the right of the archways in the shot filmed).

46. "THE WINNER"
February 26, 1971
Written by Elroy Schwartz
Directed by Robert Reed
Regulars: Reed, Henderson, Davis, McCormick, Plumb, Olsen, Williams, Knight, Lookinland
Guests: Hal Smith as ....Kartoon King
Kerry MacLane as........................... Boy

When Cindy wins a prize for being the best jacks player, Bobby starts getting an inferiority complex, as he's surrounded by his siblings' awards and trophies. He can't even beat Peter at checkers, or Jan and Marcia at ring toss. He dreams of playing in the World Series, winning a speedboat race, and setting a ski jump world record.

A student selling magazine subscriptions who comes to the door gives Bobby an idea. He starts selling subscriptions and is doing well and feeling better about himself until he

64

THE BRADY BUNCH

learns Carol and Mike called all their friends and told them
to buy magazines from Bobby. He's so upset, he throws the
order blanks at them and runs upstairs.

✿

*This is the first of four episodes directed by series star
Robert Reed.*

Hal Smith played the town drunk, Otis, on The Andy
Griffith Show, *and was a regular on* Pat Paulsen's Half a
Comedy Hour. *His most famous work is as the voice of
many well-loved Disney characters and other animated
creatures, such as Goofy, Jiminy Cricket and Winnie the
Pooh.*

47. "DOUBLE PARKED"
March 5, 1971
Written by Skip Webster
Directed by Jack Arnold
Regulars: Reed, Henderson, Davis, McCormick, Plumb, Ol-
sen, Williams, Knight, Lookinland
Guests: Jackie Coogan as...............................Man
Jack Collins as..................Mr. [Harry] Phillips

The kids are bummed because Woodland Park is being
closed. The city is putting up a building on the site. They
don't know what to do until Carol suggests they protest. The
kids give up their usual after-school activities to work the
neighborhood with a petition. Carol's women's club elects
her chair of the "Save Woodland Park" committee. She's
happy except she knows it's going to be a lot of work.

Mr. Phillips calls Mike in to tell him the good news—
they've finally gotten their first municipal contract. It's the
new courthouse building in Woodland Park and Mike's in
charge. The family is dismayed, but Mike tells them to go
ahead with their plans and the family room is turned into a
center for mass mailings, picket signs, and bumper stickers.
Their first event is a press conference on the steps of city
hall. Mr. Phillips sees seven Bradys at the forefront of the

group, and yells at Mike. He tells Mike to stop Carol or lose his job.

❀

Benedict Arnold was a traitor to the American cause during the Revolutionary War. He planned to surrender West Point to the British.

Mike calls Carol the "Joan of Arc of Woodland Park." Joan of Arc was a French heroine who took up arms while still a girl and led a battle against the English, who later captured her and burned her as a witch.

When Alice can't remember the quote, Peter does: Revolutionary War hero John Paul Jones said, "I have not yet begun to fight," as the British sunk his ship Bonhomme Richard *and demanded his surrender in 1779.*

Jackie Coogan became a star at age six, in Charlie Chaplin's The Kid. *Today, he's best remembered for his Uncle Fester on the original* Addams Family *TV series. He was also a regular on early TV's* Pantomime Quiz, Cowboy G-Men, *and* McKeever & The Colonel. *He made a number of movies, beginning with* Peck's Bad Boy *and* My Boy *in the 1920s, to* The Escape Artist *in 1982.*

48. "ALICE'S SEPTEMBER SONG"
March 12, 1971
Written by Elroy Schwartz
Directed by Oscar Rudolph
Regulars: Reed, Henderson, Davis, McCormick, Plumb, Olsen, Williams, Knight, Lookinland
Guests: Allan Melvin as ....Sam
             Steve Dunne as ....Mark Millard

Alice gets a call from a guy from her past. A guy she really liked. They make a date and that night Sam shows up. Carol asks Mike to get rid of him. But he fails and Alice is left to explain that she has another date. For a week.

Mark is pretty great-looking and he brings her flowers.

He tells her the years haven't touched her at all. She's wowed. Later, Carol and Mike get worried when Alice isn't home by 1:30 A.M. She comes in shortly, and she's waltzing on air.

The week goes extremely well. Mark has taken her to a different restaurant every night, they've been out dancing until all hours. She's in heaven. At dinner that night, he's a little vague about the business deal he's working on while in town. But he portrays it as a fabulous opportunity. He gets Alice so het up, she's drooling to give him her money.

✿

The title refers to the song by Maxwell Anderson and Kurt Weill, "September Song," which was sung by actor (later famous director) Walter Huston in their play Knickerbocker Holiday *(1938). It was selected in 1963 by ASCAP for its all-time Hit Parade, and the recording of the song by Frank Sinatra is a perennial favorite.*

49. "TELL IT LIKE IT IS"
March 26, 1971
Written by Charles Hoffman
Directed by Terry Becker
Regulars: Reed, Henderson, Davis, McCormick, Plumb, Olsen, Williams, Knight, Lookinland
Guests: Richard Simmons as .... Mr. Delafield
Jonathan Hole.................Willie Witherspoon
Elaine Swann......................Nora Maynard

Carol's acting mysteriously. Both Alice and Mike have caught her in the middle of the night writing something. Then Mike runs into Carol at a restaurant where she's lunching with Mr. Delafield, the editor of *Tomorrow's Woman* magazine. Carol's writing a story about the family for the magazine. Mike's proud and sets up his den as a workplace for her.

The kids go through the wastebaskets to get a clue to the article and prepare for being famous. Carol sends the article off and after a week, she's getting itchy to hear something. She does. It's a rejection letter.

❀

Other than the fashion magazines, there were really only two women's magazines of the type Tomorrow's Woman *is supposed to be,* Woman's Day *and* Family Circle. *As more and more women entered the workplace, these "homemaker" magazines changed and were eventually supplanted by different types of publications.*

BRADY HAIR DOS AND DON'TS

It all started with the theme song. It's certain that Sherwood Schwartz never knew what chaos he wrought when he wrote about the ladies "with hair of gold, like their mother."

Casting six kids was horrendous, but actually they had to cast twelve kids, three blonde girls, three brunettes, and the matching half-dozen boys—because they hadn't cast the parents yet.

Once it was decided to make all the women blonde, they had to be *really* blonde. Florence Henderson's hair was still quite short from her appearance in the film *The Song of Norway*. So they dumped a platinum bubble do wig on her, which she suffered through for most of the first season. Then she seems to have had a different hair color almost weekly, as the production team put her through the rinse cycle until she called a halt to it.

Susan Olsen suffered a similar fate. Not only was she

stuck with Buffy's sausage curls seemingly forever (after she made the mistake of asking her mother to make her resemble the *Family Affair* actress for Susan's *Brady Bunch* audition), she was also peroxided and tinted until she started losing her hair. The hairdressers weren't worried—Buffy's curls were fakes, and Cindy's could be too, but mercifully they stopped before Olsen was bald.

The men were not exempt. Mike Lookinland doesn't have dark hair, it's kind of reddish. It's natural in the pilot and in the later reunion shows, but the first season, you'll note his hair color changes from episode to episode and from lighting setup to lighting setup. This was the result of a variety of temporary rinses and dyes that were tried on poor Mike.

But the big joke has always been the year the Brady men got perms, but Barry Williams says it's just not so. "It looked like all the Bradys got permed there for a while. One year we came in with hair that was kind of straight and the next season, we're all with curly hair. For us, Chris and myself, it was just teenage hormones kicking in. The jury's out on Robert Reed. He tells me no and I asked him several times. We went to Hawaii and he says it was the humidity. This is what he said."

THE THIRD SEASON

1971-1972

FRIDAY NIGHTS—FALL 1971

	ABC	CBS	NBC
8:00	THE BRADY BUNCH	The Chicago Teddy Bears	The D.A.
8:30	The Partridge Family	O'Hara, U.S. Treasury	NBC World Premiere Movie
9:00	Room 222		
9:30	The Odd Couple	The New CBS Friday	
10:00	Love, American Style	Night Movie	
10:30			local

SEASON RATINGS
October 1971–April 1972

1.	All in the Family	34.0
2.	The Flip Wilson Show	28.2
3.	Marcus Welby, M.D.	27.8
4.	Gunsmoke	26.0
5.	ABC Movie of the Week	25.6
6.	Sanford and Son	25.2
7.	Mannix	24.8
8.	Funny Face	23.9
	Adam 12	23.9
10.	The Mary Tyler Moore Show	23.7
	Here's Lucy	23.7
12.	Hawaii Five-O	23.6
13.	Medical Center	23.5
14.	The NBC Mystery Movie	23.2
15.	Ironside	23.0
16.	The Partridge Family	22.6
17.	The F.B.I.	22.4
18.	The New Dick Van Dyke Show	22.2
19.	The Wonderful World of Disney	22.0
20.	Bonanza	21.9
21.	The Mod Squad	21.5
22.	Rowan & Martin's Laugh-In	21.4
23.	The Carol Burnett Show	21.2
	The Doris Day Show	21.2
25.	ABC Monday Night Football	20.9

THE WORLD
1971

- Charles Manson, Patricia Krenwinkle, and Leslie Van Houghton were convicted of the murders of Sharon Tate and six others.
- The Aswan High Dam was formally dedicated. The huge, decade-long project forever ended the annual flooding of the Nile Valley.
- Telephone service between East and West Berlin was reestablished for the first time since World War II.
- Coco Chanel, long the leader of Paris *haute couture*, died in January. Meanwhile, fashion trends were all over the map. The young and hip adopted hot pants paired with shaggy, fake-fur-lined maxi-coats, then switched to Middle Eastern–influenced caftans, then on to looks taken from *The Three Musketeers*, including plumed hats. Yves St. Laurent tried to revive 1940s elegance and line, to derisive sneers from his customers. Layering and blazers for women were in, and so was creating your own style.
- Amtrak took over operation of all U.S. passenger trains.
- The melodramatic *Love Story* was the hit film of the year. Other notable movies included *Summer of '42, Carnal Knowledge, Fiddler on the Roof, The Andromeda Strain*, and *A Clockwork Orange*.
- Soviet spacecraft *Soyuz 11* successfully docked with the orbiting Soviet space station and the cosmonauts began experiments. However, upon their return to earth, the cosmonauts died during reentry.

- Louis Armstrong, long the most famous trumpet player in the world, died in New York.
- Japanese Emperor Hirohito made the first trip abroad by a Japanese monarch ever. He was greeted in Alaska by President Nixon.
- Pop music shifted into more specialized subgroups. The composer/performers became revered, including James Taylor, Neil Young, Graham Nash, and David Crosby. There was an upsurge in female talent, led by Carole King, Joni Mitchell, Melanie, and Laura Nyro. The end of an era was signaled by the closing of Fillmore East and Fillmore West, sites of the big '60s happenings. Jim Morrison of the Doors died in Paris at age 27.
- The Pittsburgh Pirates beat the Baltimore Orioles in the World Series in seven games.
- The worst earthquake in Southern California since 1933 struck the San Fernando Valley, causing widespread destruction and 58 deaths.
- Germaine Greer led the women's lib literary movement with *The Female Eunuch*. Other acclaimed books of 1971 included Herman Wouk's *The Winds of War*, Bernard Malamud's *The Tenants*, Joyce Carol Oates's *The Onion Eaters*, and Dee Brown's *Bury My Heart at Wounded Knee*. John Lennon helped his wife, Yoko Ono, promote her book *Grapefruit*.
- Violence exploded at the New York state prison, Attica. When the smoke cleared, 42 inmates were dead.
- The UN General Assembly voted to admit China and expel Taiwan.
- Daniel Ellsberg leaked the "Pentagon Papers" to the press. The secret documents were detailed analyses of the Vietnam War.
- Two weeks of antiwar demonstrations in Washington resulted in over 10,000 arrests.
- Golfer Lee Trevino, dubbed "Super Mex," dominated professional golf in 1971, winning the British, Canadian, and U.S. Opens and winning nearly $250,000.
- Two sensations helped keep Broadway alive: a nostalgic

revamped revival of *No, No, Nanette*, starring Ruby Kee-
ler (the tap-dancing wonder of the archetypal backstage
musical film *42nd Street*) and Tim Rice and Andrew
Lloyd Webber's controversial *Jesus Christ Superstar*.
But Off-Broadway was vitally alive with acclaimed productions of *One Flew Over the Cuckoo's Nest*, *Godspell*,
and *The House of Blue Leaves*.

TELEVISION
1971

- The biggest development of the year was the first in-
  dustry-wide introduction of videocassettes and the
  equipment to play them.
- Cable TV was a burgeoning industry, with more than
  2,500 cable companies in the U.S., and the ability for
  the first time to move into large cities.
- Overseas sales of U.S. programs fell slightly, though
  Perry Mason, *Bonanza*, and *The Carol Burnett Show*
  continued to sell well overseas. Superb programming
  from British television was shown all over the world,
  including the acclaimed miniseries *The Forsyte Saga*,
  The Six Wives of Henry VIII, *Elizabeth R*, and the long-
  running series *Coronation Street*.
- The big news was the implementation of the FCC's new
  prime-time access rules, where the networks were forced
  to give up a half-hour per night and an hour on Sundays
  to local programmers. This was part of the reason that
  the number of prime-time miniseries each week was

reduced from 85 in 1966 to 48 (the other contributing factor was an increase in miniseries and specials).

- Generally, the public rejected the network's effort to inject more social relevance into programming. The viewers wanted entertainment, and the networks complied with the staples of westerns, mysteries, and comedy-variety programs which had been around for years.

- New shows for the fall season included crime dramas *Cannon, Columbo*, and *McMillan and Wife* (added to *McCloud* under a new umbrella title, *The NBC Mystery Movie*); *The D.A.*; *O'Hara, U.S. Treasury*; *Longstreet*; *Owen Marshall, Counselor at Law*; *The Persuaders*; and *Sarge*.

- The dramas fared better than the new comedies, which included *The Chicago Teddy Bears, The Partners, The Good Life, The Jimmy Stewart Show, Shirley's World*, and *The Funny Side*.

- Color TV was pervasive. Over 50 percent of U.S. homes now had color sets, and the networks and all American broadcast stations sent out nearly all programming in color.

- *Apollo 14* landed on the moon February 5 and sent back color TV pictures.

- Hugh Downs left the *Today* show after nine years as host. He was replaced by Frank McGee.

- Public access TV was first tested in New York City, during the summer, on two cable companies with a total of 80,000 subscribers. It was planned to be a community forum for ideas or information.

- Johnny Carson told NBC he wanted to move the production location of *The Tonight Show* from New York City to Los Angeles.

- CBS caused a huge controversy with a February special, "The Selling of the Pentagon." The program detailed the military's propaganda efforts to sell its policies to the American public. The show later was proved to have used shady journalistic techniques, downright lies, and other questionable practices.

THE BRADY BUNCH
1971

In the '60s and '70s, sitcoms weren't as chained to their soundstages as they are now (they weren't shot in front of a live audience for one thing, and were filmed with one camera like dramatic and adventure shows). But the Bradys went further afield than the usual backlot for its third season's opener.

The whole clan actually went to the Grand Canyon, filming a three-part story on the family vacation. The rest of the season was about the usual problems of the kids as they were becoming teenagers. There were more shows about self-image, and the kids' more adult activities, like photography, journalism, acting, and jobs.

In a move nearly unheard of in television history, ABC didn't mess with its successful Friday night comedy block led by *The Brady Bunch*. It wasn't a blockbuster, but did very well. Then come December, Norman Lear, creator of the number one show of the year, introduced another of his top ten comedies, *Sanford and Son*. NBC slotted it opposite the Bradys.

Since *Sanford and Son* was a late entry, NBC put a failed comedy opposite the Bradys that summer. *The Partners* starred Don Adams and Rupert Crosse as loony cops.

Sanford and Son, based on a British sitcom, *Steptoe and Son*, would be back in the fall, offering unbeatable competition. The show starred Redd Foxx as a junk dealer and Demond Wilson as his son and partner.

THE EPISODES

50. "GHOST TOWN USA"
September 17, 1971
Written by Howard Leeds
Directed by Oscar Rudolph
Regulars: Reed, Henderson, Davis, McCormick, Plumb, Olsen, Williams, Knight, Lookinland
Guests: Jim Backus as ....Zaccariah [T. Brown]
Hoke Howell as............ Gas Station Attendant

The whole family's dying of curiosity and Mike and Carol finally reveal the surprise: they're all going to the Grand Canyon. Mike's already got a camper hooked to the station wagon. He has the guys check all the sleeping bags, and they manage to get the family shoehorned into the car and ready to leave.

When they stop at a service station, the attendant tells them about a nearby ghost town and they decide to camp out there instead of the trailer park they were heading for. The Bradys find the ghost town and pitch camp, much to the consternation of a wizened old guy who watches from a balcony.

The family does a lot of exploring and at suppertime the old prospector makes his appearance and is offered some food. He takes the Bradys on a tour of the town and locks them in the jail. He thinks they're there to jump his claim.

❀

This episode was shot on the old Bonanza *studio set, after the western show moved to an authentically detailed Ponderosa Ranch location in Incline Village, Nevada. The new ranch was built by a developer after thousands of viewers flocked to the area looking for the Ponderosa.*

Jim Backus starred as millionaire Thurston Howell III on Sherwood Schwartz's Gilligan's Island. *His crusty old pros-*

pector here is just as well-drawn a character. He seems to truly revel in telling the kids the history of his town.

51. "GRAND CANYON OR BUST"
September 24, 1971
Written by Tam Spiva
Directed by Oscar Rudolph
Regulars: Reed, Henderson, Davis, McCormick, Plumb, Olsen, Williams, Knight, Lookinland
Guests: Jim Backus as ....Zaccariah [T. Brown]
Michele Campo as ....Jimmy

While stranded in the ghost town, Carol remembers how they got in that fix, now stranded without a car, food, or water. Mike and Peter have left, looking for help. The rest of the family decides to do what they can. Alice and the girls try to get Bessie, the donkey, to pull the plow to spell out HELP in the dirt, Carol and Cindy try to get water out of the old, dusty well, and Greg and Bobby find an old phone that they rig with their radio batteries so that it actually works. Yeah, but all it does is ring in another building in the ghost town.

The whole family's building a signal fire when Mike returns with Zaccariah and Peter. The old prospector apologizes, saying he thought they were trying to steal his claim. They're all pretty happy to leave the place.

They find a camp and then reach the Grand Canyon. The whole family's pretty awed. After a night in camp, they set out on a mule ride down to the bottom of the canyon. Only Alice is very, very dubious.

❁

Florence Henderson says, "My favorite episodes were when we went to Hawaii and the Grand Canyon and we got to go down the Grand Canyon on mule, and that was one of the scariest things in my life and when we came back up, my saddle wasn't dry." Susan Olsen adds, "I was so young, I wasn't aware. When I think of it now, I have a terrible fear of heights and I think, 'Oh, my God.' "

52. "THE BRADY BRAVES"
October 1, 1971
Written by Tam Spiva
Directed by Oscar Rudolph
Regulars: Reed, Henderson, Davis, McCormick, Plumb, Olsen, Williams, Knight, Lookinland
Guests: Jay Silverheels as .... Chief Eagle Cloud
　　　　　Michele Campo as .... Jimmy

Cindy and Bobby get separated from the rest of the Bradys and start to panic when they call and call and get no answer. They're really getting scared when they suddenly see a small Native American boy, dressed in tribal clothes. He tells them his name is Jimmy and he can show them the way to get back to the Brady camp, but won't.

Cindy and Bobby don't understand, but they like Jimmy, so they talk and finally he says he needs to be alone and away from his grandfather, and if he takes them back to the Brady camp, Cindy and Bobby's folks will return him to his grandfather. They promise they won't tell but he's sure their folks would do it anyway. But he is hungry, and when Cindy and Bobby promise to sneak him some food, he shows them the way back to camp.

Mike and Carol are incredibly relieved to find the missing kids, and later Cindy and Bobby sneak out with the food for a grateful Jimmy. But first Greg and Peter find them, then Mike, and the jig is up.

✿

The Bradys' Indian Names

Mike—Big Eagle of Large Nest
Carol—Yellow Flower with Many Petals
Greg—Stalking Wolf
Peter—Middle Buffalo/Sleeping Lizard
Cindy—Wandering Blossom
Bobby—Little Bear Who Loses Way
Jan—Dove of Morning Light
Marcia—Willow Dancing in Wind
Alice—Squaw in Waiting

53. "THE WHEELER DEALER"
October 8, 1971
Written by Bill Freeman and Ben Gershman
Directed by Jack Arnold
Regulars: Reed, Henderson, Davis, McCormick, Plumb, Olsen, Williams, Knight, Lookinland
Guests: Charlie Martin Smith as .... Ronnie
Chris Beaumont as .... Eddie

Greg's making progress on his driving. Mike's pleased, and it's a good thing since his driver's test is tomorrow. The next day comes and Greg passes his test. Now he's got to get a car of his own. He starts at the top, looking at the latest models in a magazine. He's already got $109 saved.

Greg ends up buying an old heap from a friend. He gets it home and the horn sticks, bleating like a lovesick moose and belching steam. But with the help from the rest of the kids, Greg gets the car fixed up great. Well, at least it looks great.

✿

Mike reminds Greg that his name is "Brady, not Onassis," referring to the Greek multibillionaire Aristotle Onassis, who at that time was married to Jacqueline Kennedy.

Despite its condition, the 1957 Chevy Greg buys is worth

many thousands of dollars today. When he calls it a classic, he's forecasting the future accurately.

54. "MY SISTER BENEDICT ARNOLD"
October 15, 1971
Written by Elroy Schwartz
Directed by Hal Cooper
Regulars: Reed, Henderson, Davis, McCormick, Plumb, Olsen, Williams, Knight, Lookinland
Guests: Gary Rist as ....Warren [Mulaney]
Sheri Cowart as ....Kathy [Lawrence]

Greg's sore when the coach takes him off the first-string basketball squad in favor of Warren Mulaney, who got the slot by playing politics.

Marcia's thrilled because she's got her first date with a high school hunk—Warren Mulaney.

Greg finds out when Warren comes over to pick up Marcia. He has a fit. After their date, she says he's not much different from the boys she already knows. She was going to ask him to the school carnival, but she didn't really like him enough. But before she can tell Greg, he tells her she'd better not go out with Warren again—or else.

❀

Sheri Cowart (who plays Marcia's friend Kathy here), is a musical comedy actress/dancer today. She was an Eva Perón understudy in the first national company of Evita, *played Mabel Normand in the Anthony Newley musical* Chaplin, *and appeared in* Sophisticated Ladies.

55. "THE PERSONALITY KID"
October 22, 1971
Written by Ben Starr
Directed by Oscar Rudolph
Regulars: Reed, Henderson, Davis, McCormick, Plumb, Olsen, Williams, Knight, Lookinland
Guests: Sheri Cowart as .... Kathy

Monica Ramirez as ....Kyle
Margie DeMeyer as ....Judy
Jay Kocen as ....Boy #1
Pierre A. Williams as......................Boy #2
Karen Peters as.............................Susie

Peter goes to a party where someone tells him he has no personality. He believes the kid and goes into a funk. Meanwhile, Bobby and Cindy are scouring the house for potential fire and safety hazards. They convince Mike to hold a fire drill.

The other kids try to think of a way to help Peter. Marcia and her friend Kathy try to flatter him but Cindy blows it. Then Peter turns down a party invitation because he thinks he's dull. Mike tells him to change his personality if he doesn't like it. Peter watches old movies and tries out some of the stars' mannerisms, but the British gentleman and Humphrey Bogart don't work. Then Peter tries to be a comedian, and his folks let him have a party to try out his new personality, but the kids have heard all the jokes.

✿

When Peter imitates Humphrey Bogart in this episode, he keeps repeating the menu for dinner that night in Bogart's voice, "Pork chops and applesauce." In The Brady Bunch Movie, *these words are written on the kitchen blackboard, a subtle reference to this episode.*

56. "JULIET IS THE SUN"
October 29, 1971
Written by Brad Radnitz
Directed by Jack Arnold
Regulars: Reed, Henderson, Davis, McCormick, Plumb, Olsen, Williams, Knight, Lookinland
Guests: Randy Case as .... Harold [Axelrod]
          Lois Newman as ....Miss Goodwin

Jan and Peter rush home with thrilling news—they're both in the school play, *Romeo and Juliet*. Marcia tried out for the nurse, but they haven't announced the big parts yet. Miss Goodwin calls with the news that Marcia got the role of Juliet. But Marcia doesn't want the part and Mike and Carol can't figure out why. She tells them she thinks she got the part because Carol is chairman of the play committee. Plus, she says she's not beautiful or noble enough to play Juliet.

The family tries to buck up Marcia's self-confidence and it works. By morning, she decides to accept the part. In fact, she's so stuck on herself that the Bradys are afraid they've created a monster.

❀

The title is a line from Romeo and Juliet. *Romeo Montague has met Juliet Capulet at the ball, fallen in love, and discovered she is the daughter of of his family's archenemies. The next night, he ventures into the Capulet orchard and sees Juliet in a lighted window.*

But soft! What light through yonder window breaks?
It is the east, and Juliet is the sun!
Arise, fair sun, and kill the envious moon,
That thou her maid art far more fair than she.

57. "AND NOW A WORD FROM OUR SPONSOR"
November 5, 1971
Written by Albert E. Lewin
Directed by Peter Baldwin
Regulars: Reed, Henderson, Davis, McCormick, Plumb, Olsen, Williams, Knight, Lookinland
Guests: Paul Winchell as .... Skip Farnum
Bonnie Boland as .... Myrna [Carter]
Art Lewis as .... Felder
Lennie Bremen as .... Truck Driver

The Bradys are "discovered" in a local supermarket parking lot! The director of the market's TV commercials is looking for the perfect—and natural—family to be a detergent's spokesfamily. The kids are thrilled, but Mike and Carol are a little dubious; however, they agree to do it. The director wants no rehearsal and this makes Mike and Carol worry that they're going to look like complete boobs on the tube.

So they get some coaching from an actress. She's very "method" and fills their heads with words like "motivation" and works on their projection. But this turns them into pretentious, overwrought, slick phonies.

❀

TV shows started out with just one sponsor per program, since that was common on radio. As advertisers sought more exposure, the 60-second commercial became the standard. A show seemed much less cluttered than today, when each break contains five or more spots.

The legal department must have gone nuts coming up with all the phony detergent names for use in this episode when Carol reels off the products they've used, including Clear & Bright, Help, Champ the Dirtfighter, Best, Safe, and New, Improved Safe.

When Alice says, "One brief shining moment," she's quoting a lyric from Camelot. The title song from the Lerner and Loewe musical was introduced by Richard Burton and Julie Andrews on Broadway in 1960. It was a favorite of then President John F. Kennedy.

Paul Winchell is obviously having a ball playing the hippie director in this episode. After Edgar Bergen, Winchell was the best ventriloquist around on early TV. He had polio as a child, but defeated the disease to become a performer. He debuted on TV in 1947 and went on to become a staple of prime-time variety shows, late night talk shows, and even had a children's show in the '50s.

58. "THE PRIVATE EAR"
November 12, 1971
Written by Michael Morris
Directed by Hal Cooper
Regulars: Reed, Henderson, Davis, McCormick, Plumb, Olsen, Williams, Knight, Lookinland

Marcia's in love with Andrew Whittaker. She can't wait to tell Jan (after she swears her to secrecy). She doesn't know Peter has Mike's tape recorder hidden under their bed and has recorded their whole conversation. When Peter starts giving Marcia grief about her love life and accuses Jan of telling, Jan insists she didn't tell, but Marcia doesn't believe her.

Then Greg tells Marcia that he forgot to return a library book that's *40* weeks overdue. He asks Marcia to lend him some money and makes her promise not to tell. Peter razzes Greg about the book and Greg accuses Marcia of telling.

Pretty soon, all the kids are fighting, thinking everyone's a tattler except Peter. In fact, the kids aren't speaking to each other. Any of them.

❀

The title is, of course, a twist on private eye, but it also brings to mind the avant-garde 1963 plays The Private Ear *and* The Public Eye, *which were usually performed together.*

59. "HER SISTER'S SHADOW"
November 19, 1971
Teleplay by Al Schwartz and Phil Leslie
Story by Al Schwartz and Ray Singer
Directed by Russ Mayberry
Regulars: Reed, Henderson, Davis, McCormick, Plumb, Olsen, Williams, Knight, Lookinland
Guests: Lindsay Workman as..................... Principal
             Gwen Van Dam as................... Mrs. Watson
             Peggy Doyle as............................ Teacher

Julie Reese as ....Katy
Nancy Gillette as ....Pompom Girl

Jan's doing well in her schoolwork, but not as well as her perfect sister Marcia, and it's bugging her. She comes home and in frustration, dumps all of Marcia's awards into the closet. When confronted, she gets mad. Carol and Mike finally find out Jan's sick of being in Marcia's shadow. Marcia is made editor of the school newspaper and it's one more sword through Jan. She sees a notice for pompom girl tryouts, and that's one thing Marcia never did.

✿

This episode is one of those used in the plot of 1995's The Brady Bunch Movie. *This is where Jan utters the immortal "Marcia, Marcia, Marcia" and hears voices in her head.*

Note that the judge on the end during the contest is Sherwood Schwartz's daughter, Hope Sherwood, who played Greg's girlfriend Rachel in several episodes.

60. "CLICK"
November 19, 1971
Written by Tom and Helen August
Directed by Oscar Rudolph
Regulars: Reed, Henderson, Davis, McCormick, Plumb, Olsen, Williams, Knight, Lookinland
Guests: Elvera Roussel as....................Linette Carter
Bart La Rue as...............................Coach

Greg goes home reluctantly. He screws up his courage and tries to tell Carol something but can't. Mike comes home and offers moral support. Greg finally spits it out. He made the football team. Carol says, "No son of mine is going to play football with those two-ton monsters." Mike describes all the good things about football, like teamwork and sportsmanship, and she finally gives in.

Greg gets one of the benefits of being on the team real

fast—he has Linette (the head cheerleader) over and is taking photos of her. But Greg works hard on the field, too, and gets picked for the first string for a practice game. It isn't long before he's got a fractured rib. Carol freaks out and she and Mike say no football until it's healed. Greg's not only miserable, he's sure Linette is going to dump him.

✿

Barry Williams recently commented on The Brady Bunch's *negative image, "What I don't understand is why the critics don't feel there is room for different types of programming. I've done shows that are comedic, that are farce, that are broad slapstick, that are dramatic. And our show is a type of programming. It's light, it's moralistic, it's about communication, it's about families, and it's hopefully entertaining. And I think that has its place in television."*

•

61. "GETTING DAVY JONES"
December 10, 1971
Written by Phil Leslie and Al Schwartz
Directed by Oscar Rudolph
Regulars: Reed, Henderson, Davis, McCormick, Plumb, Olsen, Williams, Knight, Lookinland
Guests: David Jones as .... [Himself]
        Britt Leach as............................. Manager
        Marcia Wallace as .... Mrs. Robbins
        Kimberly Beck as .... Laura
        Tina Andrews as ....Doreen
        Whitney Rydbeck as .... Page

Marcia's in hot water. She's president of the local Davy Jones fan club and she's in charge of the senior prom entertainment committee. When she learns Davy's in town, she's sure he'll appear at their prom since he wrote her such a nice letter. But Marcia can't penetrate the superstar's wall of security. The whole family's stumped, and Marcia's disappointed but figures she'll just get someone else, until she goes to school and finds out the rest of her committee has told the whole school that Davy's attending.

The girls notice he's on a local TV show and Mike drives Marcia to the station. But the show was taped in advance, yesterday. The rest of the kids try everything they can think of, but no one has any luck. Sam even offers his services, since he supplies meat to the hotel where the rocker is staying.

❖

Davy (David) Jones was one of the top teen heartthrobs of the time. He played a member of a rock group on a TV show about a Beatles-like band; the show caught on and the group became real. The Monkees was on the air from 1966 to 1968, and tried to capture the mod world of the Fab Four. The group split in 1969, but has recently rejoined and experienced a resurgence of interest. Jones appeared on Broadway in Oliver! *and also in* Pickwick, *and guest-starred in a number of TV series.*

The building used for the exterior establishing shot of the hotel where Jones is staying is really a condominium (then apartments) in West Hollywood. Composer Marvin Hamlisch lived there for a number of years.

This episode is one which furnishes the story for 1995's The Brady Bunch Movie. *Davy Jones again appears as himself and sings the same song, "Girl," which was written by Charles Fox and Norman Gimbel.*

62. "THE NOT-SO-ROSE-COLORED GLASSES"
December 24, 1971
Written by Bruce Howard
Directed by Leslie H. Martinson
Regulars: Reed, Henderson, Davis, McCormick, Plumb, Olsen, Williams, Knight, Lookinland
Guest: Robert Nadder as .... Mr. [Gregory] Gaylord

Mike and Carol can't understand it when they get a call from Jan's teacher (Mr. Brenner) that she stole someone else's bike. It looks just like hers, and Jan says she was just in a hurry. Mike asks her to return it fast because he's taking the kids for a photo session, so he can give Carol a family portrait for their anniversary.

As the photographer gets set, Jan nearly ruins the shot by squinting. Then they get a letter from another teacher that Jan's grades are falling off. When Carol asks Jan to read it, it's clear that she needs glasses. But Jan would rather fail school than look "positively goofy."

She gets the glasses but takes them off whenever Carol and Mike can't see her. In fact, when she goes to meet a boy at the library, she takes them off before getting on her bike. When she comes back, she crashes into the garage back wall and smashes the large framed family photo. It's ruined and the ditsy photographer has lost the negative.

❁

Sherwood Schwartz tried to give each of the characters episodes highlighting their characters. Jan, as the middle child who is reluctant to just go along with the others, was particularly rich fodder for stories. Several scenes from this episode are used as part of the plot in 1995's The Brady Bunch Movie.

63. "THE TEETER-TOTTER CAPER"
December 31, 1971
Written by Joel Kane and Jack Lloyd
Directed by Russ Mayberry
Regulars: Reed, Henderson, Davis, McCormick, Plumb, Olsen, Williams, Knight, Lookinland
Guest: Dick Winslow as.................... [Arch] Winters

Cindy and Bobby feel left out when everyone in the family but them are invited to cousin Gertrude's wedding. It seems like they're too young to do anything important. They're watching TV when they see a story about two college kids trying to set a new teeter-totter record (the old one is 124 hours). They decide to try to beat it themselves, starting the next morning.

At lunchtime, Carol's surprised they're still at it (she didn't think they were serious), and Cindy and Bobby eat their sandwiches while teetering (or tottering, as the case may be). When Mike comes home, they're still at it. The rest of the kids give them a hard time, at least until a newspaper reporter and photographer arrive.

❀

Dick Winslow, who plays the reporter, also appeared on My Favorite Martian *and* The Beverly Hillbillies.

64. "LITTLE BIG MAN"
January 7, 1972
Written by Skip Webster
Directed by Robert Reed
Regulars: Reed, Henderson, Davis, McCormick, Plumb, Olsen, Williams, Knight, Lookinland
Guest: Allan Melvin as .... Sam

Bobby is helping Greg fix a second-story shutter when Greg gets a phone call. He tells Bobby not to climb the ladder, but he does anyway. Greg comes to his rescue, and finds out his attempts stem from Bobby feeling inferior because he's short. When Sam calls him "shrimpo," insult is added to injury. Sam gives him a pep talk and cheers Bobby up. Sam also hires Greg as his new delivery boy at a buck-fifty an hour.

Bobby's still obsessing about his height, and hangs from the parallel bars, hoping he'll stretch. Marcia, Jan, and Cindy try to help by moving the mark he measures himself by, but when he finds out, he gets even more depressed and is sure he will never grow another inch.

❀

Robert Reed, despite his run-ins with the production staff, always defended the show over the years. "We were a little bit larger than life and tended to solve problems in 30 minutes, but there's nothing wrong with that. If anything, we tried to portray a family for our peer groups in a positive way, one in which they could take some little-bitty lesson perhaps. I hope so."

65. "DOUGH RE MI"
January 14, 1972
Written by Ben Starr
Directed by Allen Burton
Regulars: Reed, Henderson, Davis, McCormick, Plumb, Olsen, Williams, Knight, Lookinland
Guests: John Wheeler as .... Mr. Dimsdale
Songs: "We Can Make the World a Whole Lot Brighter"
"Time To Change"................. The Brady Kids

Greg writes a song he thinks is a guaranteed gold record, "We Can Make the World a Whole Lot Brighter." He'd love to record it, but Dimsdale's recording studio charges $150 for session time. Peter knows Dimsdale's son Johnny and he tries to get him to cut the price. He won't, but while Peter's there, he learns that family groups are hot. One was in the studio recording when he was there. And there were only five of them.

Greg goes for the idea and the Brady Six is born. In his head, anyway. Marcia and Jan aren't too wild about it, but he plays on their egos and it works. The kids all pool their money and Greg asks Mike for the rest. They're in business until Peter's voice starts changing.

✿

John Wheeler appeared on Green Acres *and* Love, American Style.

Both songs in this episode were available as singles (Paramount PAA#0141) and appear on the album Meet the Brady Bunch *(PAS 6032). "Time to Change" was also available on Paramount (PAA#0167). Greg's guitar solo of his first song was never released commercially.*

66. "JAN'S AUNT JENNY"
January 21, 1972
Written by Michael Morris
Directed by Hal Cooper
Regulars: Reed, Henderson, Davis, McCormick, Plumb, Olsen, Williams, Knight, Lookinland
Guest: Imogene Coca as........................Aunt Jenny

While going through Carol's old family photos, the girls discover Jan looks exactly like Carol's Aunt Jenny did at her age. Jan vows to send Aunt Jenny her photo and requests a current one so she knows what she'll look like in 40 years. Two weeks later, Jan gets the letter and a photo and is horrified. It isn't that Aunt Jenny is . . . ugly, or . . . anything, but she sure doesn't look like Jan wants to look at that age.

For the next couple of days, Jan alternates between tears and announcements she's considering the Peace Corps or a nunnery since she is nothing to look at. Is it any wonder Jan's not thrilled when Aunt Jenny writes that she's arriving the next day?

❀

Imogene Coca, a veteran of the early days of TV, appeared on some experimental telecasts in 1939, the year television was introduced at the New York World's Fair. Impresario and TV pioneer Max Liebman first put her together with Sid Caesar in what would become a lifelong partnership. They appeared on The Admiral Broadway Revue *followed by* Your Show of Shows. *Coca had her own comedy show in 1955, performed on many of the '50s anthology shows, as well as* Love, American Style; Trapper John, M.D.; Fantasy Island; *and* Moonlighting. *She had regular roles in* Grindl *and* It's About Time. *She's also performed on stage, including costarring in the musical comedy* On the Twentieth Century *with Rock Hudson and Madeline Kahn. She made a rare film appearance in the comedy* Under the Yum Yum Tree.

Aunt Jenny's Friends (And What They Were Doing in 1972)

Wilt Chamberlain (led Lakers basketball team to '72 championship)

Harry Houdini (legendary magician—still dead*)

Golda Meir (Prime Minister of Israel)

Pietro (?—could have originally been Pablo Picasso—famous Spanish painter living in France at the time—disguised for legal reasons**)

Indira Gandhi (Prime Minister of India)

Raquel Welch (actress filming The Last of Sheila)

Hirohito's chef (Hirohito was Emperor of Japan)

Madam Khrushchev (wife of Nikita—Soviet Premier, 1958–64)

Ari (Aristotle Onassis—Greek shipping tycoon)

Jackie (Jacqueline Kennedy Onassis—his wife, also widow of slain U.S. President John Fitzgerald Kennedy)

George Pompidou (President of France)

Jean-Claude Killy (1968 Olympic gold medal alpine skier)

Peggy Fleming (1968 Olympic gold medal figure skater)

Sir Edmund Hillary (first to climb Mr. Everest in '58, thereafter, he built and ran schools and a hospital for Himalayan Sherpa guides)

Paul Newman (filming The Sting)

*After his death in 1926, he swore to his wife he would return to life some day.

**There were several Italian painters known by the name Pietro, but they lived centuries before Jan's Aunt Jenny.

67. "THE BIG BET"
January 28, 1972
Written by Elroy Schwartz
Directed by Earl Bellamy
Regulars: Reed, Henderson, Davis, McCormick, Plumb, Olsen, Williams, Knight, Lookinland
Guest: Hope Sherwood as.......................... Rachel

Bobby's so thrilled he can do more chin-ups (5) than anyone in his class, that he can't stop crowing about it. And Greg's so irritated he can't get Bobby to shut up while he's on the phone that they make a bet: Greg will do twice as many chin-ups as Bobby. The loser will have to do everything the winner tells him for a week.

The contest is staged and Bobby does 11 chin-ups. Greg can only manage 19. He's mortified. Bobby really takes it out on Greg. He does every lousy chore around for all five of his siblings because Bobby tells him to. When Bobby demands to be taken on Greg's first date with Rachel, Greg explodes.

❀

Barry Williams talks about family dynamics, "In some ways, I got to do things on The BB that I didn't get to do at home, that is, I'm the youngest of three boys and on the show, I'm the oldest of six. So I learned all the tricks of how to take advantage and tease and get my younger siblings to do things."

68. "THE POWER OF THE PRESS"
February 4, 1972
Written by Bill Freedman and Sam Gershman
Directed by Jack Arnold
Regulars: Reed, Henderson, Davis, McCormick, Plumb, Olsen, Williams, Knight, Lookinland
Guests: Milton Parsons as ....Mr. Price
Angela Satterwhite as .... Diane
Bobby Riha as............................Harvey
Jennifer Reilly as .... Iris

The only thing standing between Peter "Scoop" Brady and the Pulitzer Prize is learning how to type. He's just been asked to write a column for the school paper and he really gets into the role. He takes everyone's pencils, carbon paper, and erasers. He's got Mike's typewriter and his old brown hat. But he's really short on ideas.

Marcia and Jan help Peter with finding topics, and Alice and Greg help him punch up his writing by putting students' names in it. This makes Peter the most popular boy in school. So popular, he's neglecting his studies and finals are fast approaching.

The lure of the press is powerful, though, and Peter neglects his schoolwork and when he has his science final and gets a "D" from one of the toughest teachers in school, he tries to work his column's magic by writing a column praising the teacher to the skies. Mike and Carol find out about the "D" and about the snow job and Peter's in trouble.

❀

Does anyone remember carbon paper? In the days before copying machines and word processors, if you wanted more than one copy of something, you had to type with carbon paper between each sheet. If you made a mistake, you had to correct each copy as well as the original.

When Carol says, "Fire when ready, Gridley," she refers to the famous words uttered in Manila Bay in 1898 by Commodore George Dewey to Captain Charles V. Gridley, aboard his ship during the Spanish-American War.

69. "SERGEANT EMMA"
February 11, 1972
Written by Harry Winkler
Directed by Jack Arnold
Regulars: Reed, Henderson, Davis, McCormick, Plumb, Olsen, Williams, Knight, Lookinland
Guest: [Ann B. Davis as .... Sergeant Emma]
Song: "The Caissons Go Rolling Along" .... Ann B. Davis

Alice is going on a week's vacation and leaves the family in the competent hands of her [identical] cousin Emma, former WAC master sergeant. All of a sudden the Brady household resembles Company B. Among the program:

> P.T. at 06:00 hours
> Inspection of quarters
> K.P.
> Laundry detail
> Latrine detail

The kids want an honorable discharge, but Mike figures they're "in for the duration." So the kids mount a secret campaign to get Emma to go A.W.O.L.

✿

When Alice refers to taking an airplane and not knowing where you'll end up, she refers to the rash of skyjackings that broke out at the time. It did seem that every commercial flight ended up in Cuba, Italy, Beirut, Bangladesh, or Syria.

Master Sergeant Emma's Mess Menu
Potatoes MacArthur
Beef Eisenhower
Succotash Pentagon

---

70. "CINDY BRADY, LADY"
February 18, 1972
Written by Al Schwartz and Larry Rhine
Directed by Hal Cooper
Regulars: Reed, Henderson, Davis, McCormick, Plumb, Olsen, Williams, Knight, Lookinland
Guest: Eric Shea as .... Tommy Jamison

Cindy's sick of everyone calling her a baby. She's determined to change her image. She does her hair and puts on Carol's dress and high heels. Then she reads a book Marcia's reading, *A Farewell to Arms*. She's really jealous that both her sisters are going places and having dates. She's thrilled when she gets a gift from a secret admirer (a candy bar).

This is followed by other gifts and notes. And then she gets a call. She doesn't know it, but it's Bobby who's been doing all these things to cheer her up. But unknowing, Cindy insists her secret admirer come over the next day. Now what's he to do?

❀

Larry Rhine also wrote for Bachelor Father *and* All in the Family.

71. "MY FAIR OPPONENT"
March 3, 1972
Written by Bernie Kahn
Directed by Peter Baldwin
Regulars: Reed, Henderson, Davis, McCormick, Plumb, Olsen, Williams, Knight, Lookinland
Guests: William Wellman, Jr., as......The Astronaut [Col. Dick Whitfield]
Debi Storm as .... Molly Webber
Lindsay Workman as................ Mr. Watkins
Suzanne Roth as .... Suzanne

Marcia comes home from school and she's livid. Her senior class has nominated Molly Webber, the shiest girl in the class, to run for hostess for the senior banquet. Marcia's mad because it was done as a joke. The other nominee is one of the most popular girls in school. Marcia decides to remake Molly and so she brings her home to study.

Marcia's successful beyond anyone's wildest dreams. She even helps Molly write her speech for the selection committee. Then the other girl has to drop out, and Marcia's chosen to run against Molly. She's about to drop out of the race when she hears the guest of honor will be a famous astronaut.

❀

When Carol calls Marcia "Professor Marcia Higgins," she's *referring to Henry Higgins, the dialect coach who re-*

makes Eliza Doolittle in My Fair Lady, *the musical based on George Bernard Shaw's play* Pygmalion. *The original Pygmalion was a woman-hating king in Greek legend. And the title of this episode is an obvious parody on* My Fair Lady.

72. "THE FENDER BENDERS"
March 10, 1972
Written by David P. Harmon
Directed by Allan Barron
Regulars: Reed, Henderson, Davis, McCormick, Plumb, Olsen, Williams, Knight, Lookinland
Guests: Jackie Coogan.........................Mr. Duggan
Robert Emhardt as.......................The Judge

Carol has an accident in the station wagon, resulting in a demolished right rear fender. Cindy, Bobby, and Marcia were witnesses and they—and Alice—think Mike's gonna blow his top. Carol doesn't. Mike takes it pretty well, and Carol says it wasn't her fault. A man backed out without looking as she was backing out and he hit her. The damage to his car was about the same, and they each agreed to fix their own cars.

But the man, Mr. Duggan, shows up with an estimate of $295 and when Mike accuses him of padding the bill; Duggan announces he will sue Carol, as it was her fault. After he leaves, Bobby and Cindy confirm that Carol didn't look before she backed out.

❁

Alice refers to several lawyer-oriented programs, including Robert Reed's own The Defenders *(Reed and E. G. Marshall played father and son lawyers);* The Bold Ones *(a trilogy show with one segment,* The Lawyers*); and* Owen Marshall, Counselor at Law, *starring Arthur Hill.*

Robert Emhardt also appeared in episodes of The Mary Tyler Moore Show, The Andy Griffith Show, Ensign O'Toole, Gomer Pyle, Please Don't Eat the Daisies, *and* The Tom Ewell Show.

THE FOURTH SEASON

1972-1973

FRIDAY NIGHTS—FALL 1972–73

	ABC	CBS	NBC
8:00	THE BRADY BUNCH	The Sonny and Cher Comedy Hour	Sanford and Son
8:30	The Partridge Family	·	The Little People
9:00	Room 222	CBS Friday Night Movie	Ghost Story
9:30	The Odd Couple		
10:00	Love, American Style		Banyon
10:30			

The Bunch. (Photo courtesy of a private collection)

Florence Henderson. (Photo courtesy of a private collection)

The girls:
Florence
Henderson,
Maureen
McCormick,
Susan Olsen,
Eve Plumb.
(Photo courtesy
of a private col-
lection)

The boys:
Robert Reed,
Christopher
Knight, Mike
Lookinland,
Barry Williams.
(Photo courtesy
of a private col-
lection)

The perfect parents. (Photo courtesy of a private collection)

Robert Reed. (Photo courtesy of a private collection)

"Marcia Gets Creamed," Maureen McCormick and Michael Gray. (Photo courtesy of a private collection)

"You're Never Too Old," Florence Henderson and Robert Reed. (Photo courtesy of a private collection)

Susan Olsen and Billy Barty on a 1972 special, *The Brady Bunch Meet ABC's Saturday Superstars*. (Photo courtesy of a private collection)

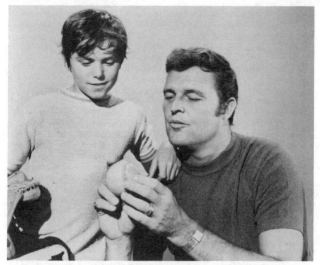

During a break filming "The Dropout," Don Drysdale, pitching ace from the L.A. Dodgers, gives Christopher Knight some tips. (Photo courtesy of a private collection)

"Dough Re Mi," Maureen McCormick and Eve Plumb. (Photo courtesy of a private collection)

"Brace Yourself," Mike Robertson and Maureen McCormick compare hardware.
(Photo courtesy of a private collection)

The Bunch as seen on Saturday morning's animated show, *The Brady Kids*.
(Photo courtesy of a private collection)

Susan Olsen, Mike Lookinland, Christopher Knight and Barry Williams make a volcano for "Today, I Am a Freshman." (Photo courtesy of a private collection)

The Bunch and Alice visit the Old West in "Bobby's Hero." (Photo courtesy of a private collection)

Greg wipes out in "Hawaii Bound," the first of three episodes shot in Hawaii at the start of the fourth season. (Photo courtesy of a private collection)

Robert Reed and the kids get ready for Easter 1972.
(Photo courtesy of a private collection)

The original Brady house in Studio City as it appears
today. (Photo courtesy of a private collection)

SEASON RATINGS
October 1972–April 1973

1.	All in the Family	33.3
2.	Sanford and Son	27.6
3.	Hawaii Five-O	25.2
4.	Maude	24.7
	Bridget Loves Bernie	24.7
6.	NBC Sunday Mystery Movie	24.2
7.	The Mary Tyler Moore Show	23.6
	Gunsmoke	23.6
9.	The Wonderful World of Disney	23.5
10.	Ironside	23.4
11.	Adam 12	23.3
12.	The Flip Wilson Show	23.1
13.	Marcus Welby, M.D.	22.9
14.	Cannon	22.4
15.	Here's Lucy	21.9
16.	The Bob Newhart Show	21.8
17.	Tuesday Movie of the Week	21.5
18.	NBC Monday Night Football	21.0
19.	The Partridge Family	20.6
	The Waltons	20.6
	Medical Center	20.6
22.	The Carol Burnett Show	20.3
23.	ABC Sunday Night Movie	20.0
	The Rookies	20.0
25.	Escape	19.9
	Barnaby Jones	19.9
	The Little People	19.9
	Wednesday Movie of the Week	19.9

THE WORLD
1972

- The controversial head of the FBI, J. Edgar Hoover, died in May. He had headed the agency since 1924, under eight presidents. Many had tried to remove him over the years but none succeeded.
- The Dallas Cowboys won the Super Bowl, defeating the Miami Dolphins 21–3.
- The McGraw-Hill publishing house announced it would not publish the highly anticipated biography of billionaire recluse Howard Hughes by Clifford Irving because they had learned it was a fraud. Later, Irving and his wife pleaded guilty in Federal Court of attempting to defraud McGraw-Hill.
- The Olympic Winter Games were held in Sapporo, Japan. The U.S.S.R. became number one in the standings with 16 gold medals.
- President Richard Nixon began his trip to China with a meeting with Communist Party Chairman Mao Tse-Tung.
- The California Supreme Court outlawed the death penalty, calling it cruel and unusual punishment.
- For reading material, Americans turned to Harold Robbins' *The Betsy*, a thinly disguised tale of Henry Ford's Tin Lizzie; Michael Crichton's *The Terminal Man*; and Roger Kahn's paean to the old Brooklyn Dodgers, *The Boys of Summer*.
- *The French Connection* won the Best Picture Oscar and

three others, including ones for Gene Hackman's performance and William Friedkin's direction. Jane Fonda won the Best Actress award for *Klute*; and the supporting awards went to Ben Johnson and Cloris Leachman for their work in *The Last Picture Show*. Charlie Chaplin returned to America for the first time in two decades to accept a special Oscar. Other big movies this year included *Cabaret, What's Up, Doc?, Man of La Mancha, The Garden of the Finzi-Continis, The Godfather, Deliverance*, and *Slaughterhouse-Five*.

- Swimmer Mark Spitz became the first athlete ever to win seven gold medals in the summer Olympiad in Munich. The next day, Palestinian terrorists broke into the Olympic village and killed 11 members of the Israeli team. The Games were suspended for 24 hours.
- President Nixon made the first official visit of a U.S. president to the U.S.S.R. He pled for peace in an unprecedented speech to the Soviet people.
- Popular music became glitzier during the year with the emergence of groups led by Alice Cooper, David Bowie, and Marc Bolan. David Cassidy's popularity soared after his exposure on *The Partridge Family*, and the younger kids mobbed Donny Osmond wherever he went. Pop invaded the theater with *Jesus Christ Superstar* and *Godspell*. The Rolling Stones toured the U.S. and Elvis Presley gave a concert at Madison Square Garden. Two novelty records made the charts—a recording of the song from the Coca-Cola commercial and one of "Amazing Grace" on bagpipes. Quadraphonic stereo was introduced and Stevie Wonder began experimenting with synthesizers.
- Bobby Fischer beat Soviet Boris Spassky to become the first American world chess champion.
- On June 17, five men were caught installing eavesdropping equipment in the Democratic National Committee headquarters in the Washington, D.C., Watergate office complex.
- President Nixon won reelection, carrying 49 states.

TELEVISION
1972

- The world's satellites were coordinated to provide global coverage of President Nixon's visits to China and the Soviet Union, the Olympics, and the various space missions. The Olympics alone sent over a thousand hours of coverage via satellite.
- There were nearly 100 million TV sets in the world by 1972 and television broadcasts were available nearly everywhere except South Africa, which planned to start a television system in 1975.
- The FCC passed new regulations governing cable TV, to increase its usage outside of rural areas, but to keep it out of major metropolitan areas.
- After public television broadcast anti-war films and a nude ballet, President Nixon vetoed a bill authorizing new funds for the Corporation for Public Broadcasting.
- By the middle of the year, challenges to license renewal were lodged against over 100 stations by minority groups who claimed their interests were being ignored by television.
- The popularity of U.S. television programming in other countries—particularly mysteries, sitcoms and westerns—continued unabated but sales dropped slightly as foreign countries gained more experience in programming and increasingly broadcast home-grown product.
- Programming moved further toward social commentary and real-life, contemporary issues during the year, reflected in the popularity of *Maude* and *Bridget Loves Bernie*. Topics recently taboo on TV (such as abortion, homosexuality, and drug abuse) were addressed on many episodic series for the first time.

- The prime-time access rules continued to be controversial in their second year. The bottom line was that off-network reruns produced significantly better ratings than station-produced original programming.
- Despite government efforts to limit it, cable and Pay-TV became larger threats to broadcasters. CATV, which stood for Community Antenna TV, moved from rural, zero-broadcast-reception areas into smaller cities and their reception was better than in major metro areas, which had more and more tall buildings interfering with signals. Soon viewers in big cities were clamoring for cable TV.
- The Philips Corp. introduced the first VLP (video long-playing) machine, which used a laser beam to decode audio and video information from a disc.
- The fall 1972 season had fewer new shows than usual, but several of these were the "wheel" shows which alternated different series from week to week. It also promised a lot more specials and public affairs programs.
- NBC had to cope with the death of Dan Blocker, star of its long-running *Bonanza*. It was decided not to replace him, but they added a couple of ranch hands. The show was moved from its traditional Sunday slot to Tuesday nights, where it quietly expired in January. After fourteen years, many of them in the top ten, *Bonanza,* like Dan Blocker, was gone.

THE BRADY BUNCH
1972

The season began with the ultimate adventure—the Bradys in Hawaii. Greg gets to surf, and the rest of the family comes back with great tans. In fact Maureen's is visible for several episodes after their return.

This was a season of teenage problems. Not only Barry and Maureen, but Eve and Chris all were quite grown up by this year. So Marcia falls for an older man, Peter falls for lots of girls, Greg struggles in the abyss between youth and adulthood, and all the kids start thinking about ways to make money, what careers they'll eventually pursue, and success.

But the show that has become a Brady touchstone is "Amateur Nite," where the Brady kids formed a rock group and competed directly with the Partridges and Sonny and Cher. Barry Williams remembers the beginnings. "The singing and dancing kind of evolved. Back then, the Cowsills were popular, the Osmonds were popular, the Partridge Family had come out, and we liked to sing and dance just by what our sort of limited abilities were."

This generated several nationwide tours of the Brady Kids, and several albums, and Barry Williams became something of a teen idol on a par with Desi Arnaz, Jr., and David Cassidy.

THE EPISODES

73. "HAWAII BOUND"
September 22, 1972
Written by Tam Spiva
Directed by Jack Arnold
Regulars: Reed, Henderson, Davis, McCormick, Plumb, Olsen, Williams, Knight, Lookinland
Guests: Don Ho as ....[Himself]
Sam Kapu as ....[Himself—uncredited]
David "Lippy" Espinda as .... Hanalei
Dennis M. Chun as .... Young Workman
Elithe Aguiar as ....Hula Instructor
Patrick Adiarte as .... David
Songs: "Sweet Someone" ....Don Ho and Sam Kapu
"Lovely Hula Hands"................. Instrumental

Mike comes home with the surprise of a lifetime for the family. Mr. Phillips asked him to check on a building he designed—in Hawaii. And the whole family is going along. They arrive and are met by David, a representative from the construction company. He offers to take the family sightseeing over the weekend before Mike starts work.

They go on an outrigger canoe, to Pearl Harbor, and to the Arizona Memorial. Meanwhile, on the construction site, one of the workers uncovers a small idol. Another worker warns he shouldn't touch it, but the younger man tosses it aside with his shovel. When the Brady kids explore the construction site, Bobby finds the idol and decides to wear it around his neck. But later he drops it and Alice finds it. She eventually passes it on to Greg. Bobby thinks it's a good-luck charm, but bad things keep happening to whichever of them is wearing it.

❀

No one could be more associated with the '60s and '70s in Hawaii than Don Ho. First discovered by the Mainland college coeds who used to come to the University of Hawaii for low-impact summer school, Ho originally performed at his mother's place, Honey's, on the windward side of Oahu. As his popularity grew, he joined up with a band called the Aliis, and packed 'em in for years at a large club in Waikiki's International Marketplace called Duke Kahanamoku's. His recordings of "Tiny Bubbles" and "Pearly Shells" became international hits, and he made many concert tours to the Mainland. Ho eventually split with the Aliis and became a long-time attraction at the dome-shaped arena in the Hilton Hawaiian Village Hotel. Ho usually had a young, unknown singer in his act, and was responsible for launching several careers. Sam Kapu was one of them, and he went on to make several recordings and become a popular Waikiki performer on his own.

The practice of giving leis to everyone coming off a plane or a ship ended in the '50s, when tourism skyrocketed. They also used to pass out free pineapple juice at the airport, a custom discontinued in the '70s.

The song playing for the women's hula lesson is "Lovely Hula Hands," one of the traditional songs generally used for teaching tourists the hula. The music playing while Greg learns to surf is a rip-off of the theme from the long-running CBS-TV show shot in Honolulu, Hawaii Five-O.

The gold-cloaked statue the Bradys stand in front of while David talks about Iolani Palace and the new state building is the first man to unite the islands, King Kamehameha I.

74. "PASS THE TABU"
September 29, 1972
Written by Tam Spiva
Directed by Jack Arnold
Regulars: Reed, Henderson, Davis, McCormick, Plumb, Olsen, Williams, Knight, Lookinland
Guests: David "Lippy" Espinda as .... Hanalei

Cris Callow as............................ Mandy
Patrick Adiarte as .... David

Despite Greg's wipeout while surfing, Bobby thinks he might have drowned if he hadn't been wearing the idol Bobby found in Episode 73. But Greg's lost it in the surf. Amazingly, Jan finds the idol as it comes in several waves later, and sticks it in her bag.

The family goes on a picnic to Hanauma Bay (though Greg decides to stay behind and check out the Waikiki Beach babes). While the kids are swimming, a huge spider crawls into Jan's bag. Later, back at Waikiki Beach, Jan gives the tiki back to Bobby, who's with David and Greg. David says the tiki is tabu, or forbidden, and bad luck. That night, Bobby decides he doesn't want the idol and gives it to Peter.

The huge spider escapes from Jan's bag and in the middle of the night crawls up on Peter's bed. He awakens to find himself eye to eye with the spider—and he freaks.

✿

Lippy Espinda was a local Honolulu treasure. He owned a large used-car lot and became well-known for his pervasive TV ads. He occasionally acted, appearing in Hawaii Five-O *and many other productions shot in the Islands.*

Patrick Adiarte, who plays David, was the original crown prince in the film The King and I, *taking over the rule of Siam when his father (played by Yul Brynner) dies at the end of the movie. He has acted on and off during the ensuing years, appearing in several episodes of* M*A*S*H *and a number of other series. He lives in Los Angeles, is an accomplished photographer, and was married for many years to Loni Ackerman, who headed the first national company of* Evita.

The gorgeous bay where the family picnics is Hanauma Bay, near Koko Head. It was originally a volcano, then a crater (like Diamond Head). The pounding of the sea eventually opened one end, making it into the bay it is today. One of the most scenic spots on the island, it became

*so popular that the local flora and fauna are endangered
and the bay has been closed to the public to allow the ec-
osystem to regenerate.*

75. "THE TIKI CAVES"
October 6, 1972
Written by Tam Spiva
Directed by Jack Arnold
Regulars: Reed, Henderson, Davis, McCormick, Plumb, Ol-
  sen, Williams, Knight, Lookinland
Guests: Vincent Price as....Professor [Hubert] Whitehead
        David "Lippy" Espinda as .... Hanalei
        Leon Lontoc as............Mayor's Representative

Greg, Peter, and Bobby decide to follow the advice of old
Mr. Hanalei and return the idol to the ancient burial cave
of the first king. They tell Mike and Carol they're going sightseeing and creep through a spooky forest, looking for the
king's tomb. They don't know that a strange archeologist is
working in the cave and he tries scaring them away, but
they run in the wrong direction.
    He finds, threatens, and finally captures them, then ties
them up. They tell him they're trying to return the idol,
which they found in Honolulu, and they try to give him the
idol, but the loony professor insists they found it in the cave
and demands to know where.

✿

*Vincent Price was just coming into his own as king of the
"B" horror flicks and would have frightened a bunch of kids
easily. In real life, he was a highly educated, widely traveled
art, wine, and food connoisseur, who wrote a number of
books and began his acting career on the London stage,
moving to films in 1938. His most famous pictures include*
The Fly, House on Haunted Hill, House of Wax, *and* The
House of Usher.

*The luau sequence (and probably the cave scenes) look
like they were shot on the soundstage back at the Paramount lot. Note the fake leis everyone wears, made of wood*

fiber squares that were a popular craft item at the time. The Tahitian dancers are, however, first-rate and the dance they do is authentic.

76. "TODAY I AM A FRESHMAN"
October 13, 1972
Written by William Raynor and Miles Wilder
Directed by Hal Cooper
Regulars: Reed, Henderson, Davis, McCormick, Plumb, Olsen, Williams, Knight, Lookinland
Guests: John Howard as .... Doctor
Vickie Cos as .... Kim
Kelly Flynn as .... Tom
John Reilly as .... Dick

Marcia's so unnerved by her first day of high school that she can't face it and plays sick. Carol calls the doctor, who thinks it might be "new school-itis." Mike and Carol pry her fears out of her that night. She was a big cheese at Fillmore Junior High, and she isn't looking forward to being a nobody at Westdale High.

When she finally goes, she decides to act as sophisticated as possible so the other kids won't think she's juvenile. But they just think she's weird. She comes home in tears.

✿

Marcia's Clubs
Scuba
Archery
Karate
Ceramics
Stamp Collecting
Drama
Yoga
Westdale Boosters

When Alice thinks Marcia in her scuba gear is "The Creature from the Black Lagoon," she refers to the 1954 monster movie, coincidentally directed by frequent Brady Bunch *director Jack Arnold.*

77. "CYRANO DE BRADY"
October 20, 1972
Written by Skip Webster
Directed by Hal Cooper
Regulars: Reed, Henderson, Davis, McCormick, Plumb, Olsen, Williams, Knight, Lookinland
Guest: Kym Karath as....................Kerry [Hathaway]

When Peter meets Jan's new friend Kerry Hathaway, it's love at first sight. He tries to get Jan's help, but she tells him just to give Kerry a call. He does and blows it. Then he gets dressed up for school the next day, finds Kerry, drops her books in the mud, and splatters her with water from the drinking fountain.

That night, Mike says that when he was tongue-tied with a girl, he'd write her a letter. Pete gives it a try, but can't come up with much. Alice starts quoting poetry and Peter writes it down. It's a success but Pete forgets to sign the note. Then he gets a copy of *Cyrano de Bergerac*, and begs Greg to be his Cyrano, feeding him cool lines as he woos the fair Kerry at her bedroom window. But it backfires, Kerry comes outside, and thinks it's Greg who's using Peter to speak for him.

❀

Cyrano de Bergerac is the title character in an 1897 French drama by Edmond Rostand. The now-classic story concerns a romantic poet who woos the fair Roxanne for his tongue-tied friend. Cyrano had an exceedingly large nose and had given up finding romance for himself, yet falls for his friend's lady love. Cyrano was a real person, a 17th-century poet. The story has been filmed multiple times, most recently as the modernized Roxanne, *starring Steve Martin.*

78. "FRIGHT NIGHT"
October 27, 1972
Written by Brad Radnitz
Directed by Jerry London
Regulars: Reed, Henderson, Davis, McCormick, Plumb, Olsen, Williams, Knight, Lookinland

It was a dark and stormy night at the Brady's, and Cindy's sure someone's in the attic. She wakes Jan and they see a ghostly apparition in the backyard. Mike and Carol promise to check the attic, where they find an open window blowing a creaking rocking chair. But in the boys' room, there's glee, as they've pulled off another one against the girls.

But Mike and Carol—and Marcia—have figured it out. Marcia, Jan, and Cindy find the slide projector under Greg's bed, with a slide of the ghost in it. And Marcia thinks they made the rocking chair move with a rope. At dinner, the girls profess to still be scared and bet the boys their allowances they can't spend the night in the attic.

✿

They should have shot a few more feet of film when doing all the different angle shots of the Brady house exterior back in 1969. Note the hundredth time the same blue Toronado goes by the house. Perhaps it's Mr. Dittmeyer.

79. "THE SHOW MUST GO ON?"
November 3, 1972
Written by Harry Winkler
Directed by Jack Donohue
Regulars: Reed, Henderson, Davis, McCormick, Plumb, Olsen, Williams, Knight, Lookinland
Guests: Allan Melvin as .... Sam
Barbara Morrison as .... Mrs. Tuttle
Brandy Carson as .... Woman
Karen Foulkes as ....: ..... Muriel
Frank DeVol as............................. Father
Bonnie Ludeka as .... Daughter
Songs: "That Old Black Magic" .... Instrumental

"Together Wherever We Go" . . . . Carol and
Marcia Brady

Marcia wants Carol to sing a duet with her at her school's
family night, but Carol doesn't want to sing in front of all
the other mothers. Greg says practically none of the parents
want to participate, and he and Mike shame her into it. Now
the rest of the family goes out to sell tickets to the event.

Sam promises to sell tickets at his meat shop, but Alice is
really peeved that he won't go to the event with her because
he has bowling practice.

Then Greg promises he'll coerce Mike into doing an act
with him. Mike complains he has no talent, but Greg already told Mrs. Tuttle that and she suggested a dramatic
reading with Greg accompanying him on the guitar. But the
poem is a real yawn.

❁

*"Together Wherever We Go" is from the Stephen Sond-
heim–Jule Style musical* Gypsy *(1959) and was introduced
by Ethel Merman, Sandra Church, and Jack Klugman. The
version with Maureen McCormick and Florence Henderson
from this episode was never recorded, but Florence Henderson does appear on an album called* Selections from
Gypsy *and* Flower Drum Song *(RCA Camden # CAL 560).*

*When Carol says the Family Frolics was a "really big
shew," she's doing the standard imitation of the host of the
long-running Sunday night institution,* The Ed Sullivan
Show.

*The hapless father in the dreadful trumpet duet is none
other than the show's musical director, Frank DeVol.*

80. "JAN, THE ONLY CHILD"
November 11, 1972
Written by Al Schwartz and Ralph Goodman
Directed by Roger Duchowney
Regulars: Reed, Henderson, Davis, McCormick, Plumb, Ol-
sen, Williams, Knight, Lookinland

Poor Jan. She can't get into the bathroom, Marcia takes her bike, she can't even watch a movie on TV without somebody marching in and changing the channel. She gets mad and tells everyone she wishes she was an only child. Her friend Donna (an only child) seems to have a much better life. In fact, she's invited Jan to stay over Saturday night and she wants to go, even though her own family is all going to a charity hoedown. Mike asks the other kids to humor her a little.

Jan's a little bewildered at the way everybody's giving way for her and being considerate, and Cindy finally tells. She really blows up at the kids. They tell her that from now on, they're not related. She can secede from the family for all they care.

❀

This is the episode with the potato sack race, which is used in The Brady Bunch Movie.

81. "CAREER FEVER"
November 17, 1972
Written by Burt and Adele Styler
Directed by Jerry London
Regulars: Reed, Henderson, Davis, McCormick, Plumb, Olsen, Williams, Knight, Lookinland

While getting some help on her geometry homework, Marcia finds a composition Greg wrote for English class on careers. It's all about Greg's desire to be an architect, and Marcia's reading aloud when Mike comes in. He's pleased and flattered and tells Greg he'll definitely arrange for him to have a job at Mike's firm this summer. He walks out, beaming. But Greg confesses to Marcia he doesn't know what he wants to be, and only wrote that because he couldn't think of anything else.

Jan and Peter are inspired to think about their own career paths—he wants to be a doctor and Jan a nurse. Greg doesn't have the heart to tell Mike the truth, so he designs a very weird house (with a moat) and shows it to his speech-less father. But far be it from Mike Brady to discourage any of his kids.

✿

When Mike says Greg is like Frank Lloyd Wrong, he makes a joke on the name of probably the most revered architect ever, Frank Lloyd Wright. The Wisconsin-born visionary began his practice in the Chicago area, designing public and private buildings in a style which anticipated the International Style, Bauhaus, Art Moderne, and others years in the future. His early work is close to what we call the Arts and Crafts Style today, his later work in Southern California and elsewhere, Art Deco. Many of his buildings seem integral with their sites—as natural and inevitable as the boulders, streams or earth they lie upon.

82. "GOODBYE, ALICE, HELLO"
November 24, 1972
Written by Milt Rosen
Directed by George Tyne
Regulars: Reed, Henderson, Davis, McCormick, Plumb, Olsen, Williams, Knight, Lookinland
Guests: Mary Treen as . . . . .Kay
Snag Werris as . . . . .Mr. Foster
Harry G. Crigger as . . . . Customer

After Greg, Peter, and Bobby break an antique lamp, Alice swears she won't tell Carol, but upon direct grilling, she caves in. The guys are really angry that she squealed on them. Then Carol asks who was using the record player the night before and Alice innocently answers, "Marcia," who then gets her stereo privileges taken away for leaving it on all night. So the female Bradys also feel Alice can't be trusted.

Alice goes to see her friend Kay in tears because the kids are all giving her the cold shoulder. She begs Kay to fill in for her until she can decide what to do. Alice immediately tells Carol she's leaving for good, and by the time the kids get home from school she's gone.

❀

Mary Treen was a regular on a couple of early TV shows, Willy *and* The Joey Bishop Show.

83. "GREG'S TRIANGLE"
December 8, 1972
Written by Bill Freedman and Ben Gershman
Directed by Richard Michaels
Regulars: Reed, Henderson, Davis, McCormick, Plumb, Olsen, Williams, Knight, Lookinland
Guests: Tannis G. Montgomery as ......Jennifer [Nichols]
        Rita Wilson as.......................... Pat [Conway]

Greg meets the cutest girl in school. She's wowed that he's a surfer and asks him to teach her. He's thrilled. In fact, he's nearly catatonic. He reneges on a golf game with his dad and puts his math books in the refrigerator. Meanwhile, Marcia's competing for head cheerleader and Greg's on the selection committee.

Of course, what Greg doesn't know is that Jennifer is also trying out for head cheerleader. Could it be that she's only dating Greg to influence the vote? Naaaah. But Marcia sure thinks so.

❀

Rita Wilson, the cheerleader contestant who's so very good (and pretty), is now Mrs. Tom Hanks. Tannis Montgomery appeared on Happy Days, *as a love interest for Ron Howard's Richie Cunningham.*

84. "EVERYONE CAN'T BE GEORGE WASHINGTON"
December 22, 1972
Written by Sam Locke and Milton Pascal
Directed by Richard Michaels
Regulars: Reed, Henderson, Davis, McCormick, Plumb, Olsen, Williams, Knight, Lookinland

Guests: Sara Seegar as .... Miss Bailey
Barbara Bernstein as .... Peggy
Jimmy Bracken as .... Freddie
Sean Kelly as .... Stuart
Michael Barbera as .... Harvey
Cheryl Beth Jacobs as .... Edith
Angela B. Satterwhite as .... Donna

Peter's up for the part of George Washington in the school play. Jan is chosen to do the sets (because of her architect father), but Peter is depressed because Miss Bailey wants him to play Benedict Arnold. Carol talks him into doing it, but playing the most famous traitor of them all is playing havoc with his school social life as his friends equate the boy with the role.

Peter tries desperately to get dumped from the play by forgetting his lines, but Miss Bailey pastes his lines on a prop. Then he pretends to twist his ankle, but Benedict Arnold had a real limp. He tries laryngitis, then the play is canceled, disappointing everyone.

❀

Sara Seeger was a regular on two series, Dennis the Menace *(playing the second Mrs. Wilson) and* Occasional Wife, *the charming '60s sitcom starring Patricia Harty and Michael Callan. Barbara Bernstein, Florence Henderson's real-life daughter, makes her second Brady appearance in this episode.*

85. "LOVE AND THE OLDER MAN"
January 5, 1973
Written by Martin A. Ragaway
Directed by George Tyne
Regulars: Reed, Henderson, Davis, McCormick, Plumb, Olsen, Williams, Knight, Lookinland
Guests: Don Brit Reid as .... Dr. [Stanley] Vogel
Allen Joseph as .... The Minister

Marcia's walking on air after a visit to the dentist. This star-tling event baffles Carol and Alice. Their regular dentist is on vacation and his replacement is a young, groovy hunk, and Marcia's thrilled she gets to go back on Thursday for a filling. Jan reads in a teen magazine that marriage with an older man is desirable, and Marcia thinks it's a great idea.

Mike's also got an appointment and likes Dr. Vogel too. He mentions Marcia thinks he's groovy, and Dr. Vogel says he thinks Marcia's special too. In fact, does she do baby-sitting? He has a three-year old, and he and his wife would like to go to the ballet Friday night. This all gets commu-nicated to Marcia in a garbled way, so she thinks he's asked *her* to the ballet.

✿

George "Buddy" Tyne is an accomplished director of comedy, and helmed a number of episodes of M*A*S*H. He began as an actor, and had a featured role in the com-pany of the infamous production of Orson Welles's 1937 Mercury Theatre production of The Cradle Will Rock. *The revolutionary (and slightly socialist) musical inspired such violent emotions that an injunction prevented the actors and musicians from performing on stage and in the pit. Led by composer Marc Blitzstein pushing a piano, the cast and audience marched 20 blocks to a theater hastily rented by company member John Houseman, where the performance was given, with the actors performing their roles from seats in the audience and the composer playing a lone piano.*

86. "LAW AND DISORDER"
January 12, 1973
Written by Elroy Schwartz
Directed by Hal Cooper
Regulars: Reed, Henderson, Davis, McCormick, Plumb, Ol-sen, Williams, Knight, Lookinland
Guests: Shawn Schepps as ....Jill
Harlen Carraher as...........................Steve
Cindy Henderson as .... Girl
Jon Hayes as ....Jon

Everybody's avoiding Bobby like the plague. Only Cindy will walk home with him. He's been made a safety monitor, the "class cop," and he hates it. All his friends think he's the class snitch.

Meanwhile, Mike brings home a battered dinghy a client gave him. Bobby can't even help work on it because he's taking his job so seriously. Cindy's peeved when he reports her for running through the hall. Then Bobby starts playing safety monitor at home and the rest of the kids get very annoyed. In fact, when the boat's finished, none of the kids wants to go to the launch if Bobby will be there.

✿

Elements of this episode are used in the story of The Brady Bunch Movie.

Carol calls Bobby's school Clinton Avenue Elementary, though it's already been established that the name of their street is Clinton Way. Of course, there could be streets of both names in Mr. Schwartz's mythical world.

87. "GREG GETS GROUNDED"
January 19, 1973
Written by Elroy Schwartz
Directed by Jack Arnold
Regulars: Reed, Henderson, Davis, McCormick, Plumb, Olsen, Williams, Knight, Lookinland
Guests: Gracia Lee as ....Jenny
         Hope Sherwood as.........................Rachel

While taking Bobby to get a frog to enter a frog-jumping contest, Greg nearly gets into an accident. When Carol and Mike hear about it, they take away Greg's driving privileges for one week. He's in a real dilemma, because he invited Rachel to a concert and the music stores are all out of tickets. The only place that has any tickets is the arena, and Greg can't find anyone to take him there.

Finally Greg finds a sick friend who offers to loan him his car. But he gets caught when Carol runs into the friend's mother at the market. Mike confines Greg to the house for ten days, only allowing him to leave the house for school.

✿

On Susan Olsen's excellent 1995 TV special, The Brady Bunch Home Movies, *Chris Knight remembers this episode vividly and that Maureen McCormick hated the frog. "The rest of the afternoon I was carrying the frog around, trying to chase her and trying to put it on her head, and she was just beside herself with fear of a frog."*

88. "AMATEUR NITE"
January 26, 1973
Written by Sam Locke and Milton Pascal
Directed by Jack Arnold
Regulars: Reed, Henderson, Davis, McCormick, Plumb, Olsen, Williams, Knight, Lookinland
Guests: Harold Peary as ....Mr. Goodbody
          Steve Dunne as ....Pete Sterne
          Robert Nadder as ....Alfred Bailey
Songs: "It's a Sunshine Day" .... The Brady Kids
        "Keep On" .... The Brady Kids

Jan goes to collect a silver platter the kids ordered for Mike and Carol's anniversary. It has all their names and a sentiment on it. The salesman reminds Jan the engraving was extra. She thought it would be 85¢ extra, but it was *per letter.* The bill's $56.23. The kids have a week to find the money. The engraving was Jan's idea and her mistake. What now?

Cindy and Bobby go to a bank, but they've got no collateral. Jan has an idea: the kids will put together an act for The Pete Sterne Amateur Night contest. The prize is $100. The hardest part is that they have to hide their rehearsals from Mike, Carol, and Alice.

✿

Harold Peary, who plays the bank loan officer Mr. Goodbody, played The Great Gildersleeve *on the radio. The character originated on one of the most popular radio pro-*

grams, Fibber McGee and Molly. *His laugh, which he uses in this episode, was famous.*

The building used for the exterior establishing shot of the television studio was of the Metromedia independent TV station, KTTV (Channel 11) in L.A.

Both songs (and the plot) in this episode are used in 1995's The Brady Bunch Movie. *The songs have recently been re-released on a new CD,* It's a Sunshine Day: The Best of the Brady Bunch *(MCAD 10764). The original tracks are also used in the new film and are on the soundtrack.*

89. "BOBBY'S HERO"
February 2, 1973
Written by Michael Morris
Directed by Leslie H. Martinson
Regulars: Reed, Henderson, Davis, McCormick, Plumb, Olsen, Williams, Knight, Lookinland
Guests: Burt Mustin as......................Jethroe Collins
       Richard Carlyle as......................Mr. Hillary
       Gordon DeVol as ....Jesse James
       Ruth Anson as......................... Miss Perry

Bobby writes a school paper about Jesse James, and Mr. Hillary, his principal, is concerned about his glorification of an evil hero and all-around bad guy. He doesn't blame Bobby because the movies and press romanticize bad guys, but his teacher has also confiscated Bobby's cap gun. Mike and Carol try to nip their incipient James idolater in the bud, but soon he wants to watch a movie about his hero. His folks say no, until they realize James kills dozens of people in the film.

They all watch it together, but every single scene where James kills innocent bystanders has been edited out. Mike is determined to make Bobby face the truth about the James gang.

✿

Burt Mustin was a late-in-life actor, beginning his career at age 67, after a lifetime career as a car salesman (which, some would say, requires a fair amount of acting). He was over 90 when he appeared as a regular on Phyllis, *playing the beau of crotchety old Mother Dexter. He was also a regular on the early Betty White show* Date with the Angels, Ichabod and Me, The Andy Griffith Show, *and* All in the Family. *He also costarred on an interesting NBC sketch comedy show,* The Funny Side, *which featured six couples of varying ages. Mustin was paired with veteran actress Queenie Smith and the others were John Amos and Teresa Graves, Warren Berlinger and Pat Finley, Dick Clair and Jenna McMahon, and Michael Lembeck and Cindy Williams.*

90. "THE SUBJECT WAS NOSES"
February 9, 1973
Written by Al Schwartz and Larry Rhine
Directed by Jack Arnold
Regulars: Reed, Henderson, Davis, McCormick, Plumb, Olsen, Williams, Knight, Lookinland
Guests: Nicholas Hammond as ....Doug Simpson
Stuart Getz as ....Charlie
Lisa Eilbacher as ....Vicki

Marcia's got a dilemma. Big man on campus Doug Simpson asks her out for Saturday night and she accepts, forgetting she's already got a date with Charlie, a nice but unimpressive boy whose father owns a wallpaper store.

When Marcia asks Greg how to break a date with the nerdish Charlie, he tells her to use the phrase the guys all use, "Something suddenly came up." She breaks her date with him, but she feels rotten. However, when she talks to Doug, some of that rotten feeling goes away. Then Marcia calls Peter and Bobby for dinner and is hit in the nose with their football. Her nose swells up and looks horrible.

Mike and Carol try to take her mind off her nose by enlisting the whole family in a project painting their bedroom.

But the next day at school, Doug sees Marcia's nose and breaks their date for Saturday.

❀

The title brings to mind the 1965 Frank Gilroy play The Subject Was Roses. *The play won a Pulitzer and the Tony Award as Best Play.*

Lisa Eilbacher has made the difficult transition from child to adult actor and is probably best known for her role in An Officer and a Gentleman. *Her part in this episode is cut in syndication broadcasts.*

91. "HOW TO SUCCEED IN BUSINESS?"
February 23, 1973
Written by Gene Thompson
Directed by Robert Reed
Regulars: Reed, Henderson, Davis, McCormick, Plumb, Olsen, Williams, Knight, Lookinland
Guests: Jay Novello as......................Mr. Martinelli
Harlen Carraher as............. Leon [uncredited]
Claudio Martinez as ....Billy [uncredited]

Peter gets a job fixing bicycles at Mr. Martinelli's bike shop, but his mechanical abilities are less than stellar (odd, considering his plumbing skill in "The Great Earring Caper"). Poor Mr. Martinelli tells him he might be a better salesman than mechanic and Peter thinks this means he's being promoted. He passes the news along at home, but that afternoon Mr. Martinelli fires him because he spent three days working on just one bike with a minor problem.

He puts off telling Mike and Carol until after dinner, but then Alice brings out a cake celebrating his promotion. Now how does he tell them he's been fired? The next day, he asks Mr. Martinelli to take him back, but the proprietor refuses. Then when Marcia, Cindy, and Jan arrive to buy a horn, Martinelli covers for Peter. That night, Peter tries to tell his folks, but they interrupt with the news they're going to buy bicycles and he can get credit for selling them.

❀

The title brings to mind a hit Broadway musical of the time, How to Succeed in Business Without Really Trying *(1961). It used a unique plot device: the musical was an original story, whose lead character, J. Pierpont Finch (played superbly by Robert Morse), progressed through the world of big business by following the advice from the only slightly tongue-in-cheek book of the same title. The show was made into a film in 1967, also starring Morse. The music was by Frank Loesser* (Guys and Dolls) *and the choreography by Bob Fosse* (All That Jazz). *An acclaimed revival of the show, starring Matthew Broderick, opened recently on Broadway and then on national tour.*

Additional scenes with the characters of Leon and Billy were either left on the editing room floor or cut in syndication, and they are uncredited at the end of the episode. The credit does appear in two of the books on the show, so they may have been evident at some point. Perhaps they will materialize if Columbia House issues the episode uncut.

92. "THE GREAT EARRING CAPER"
March 2, 1973
Written by Larry Rhine and Al Schwartz
Directed by Leslie H. Martinson
Regulars: Reed, Henderson, Davis, McCormick, Plumb, Olsen, Williams, Knight, Lookinland

After Marcia and Jan admire Carol's new earrings, Cindy tries them on and, when about to be caught, hides them under a towel in the bathroom and flees. Alice comes in and sweeps all the dirty towels into the laundry basket, and the game's afoot.

Peter, proud possessor of a new detecting kit, plays Sherlock Holmes, detecting clues and taking fingerprints all over the place, deerstalker cap and magnifying glass firmly in place.

Meanwhile, Mike and Carol are going to a costume party and after some discussion, they decide to go as Marc Antony and Cleopatra. Carol thinks the earrings will be the perfect accompaniment to her costume.

✿

In 1973, "The _____Caper" was already a slightly tired phrase. There was a 1957 film, The Big Caper, *followed by the TV series* 77 Sunset Strip *(1958–64), which entitled many of its episodes this way. The first was "The Iron Curtain Caper," the last, "The Checkmate Caper." This inspired further caper films, such as Michael Caine's* Gambit *(1966),* The Cary Grant–Audrey Hepburn Charade *(1963), and 1972's* The Hot Rock. *Doris Day even made an album in the '60s called "Cuttin' Capers."*

93. "YOU'RE NEVER TOO OLD"
March 9, 1973
Written by Ben Gershman and Bill Freedman
Directed by Bruce Bilson
Regulars: Reed, Henderson, Davis, McCormick, Plumb, Olsen, Williams, Knight, Lookinland
Guests: Florence Henderson as .... Grandma [Connie] Hutchins
Robert Reed as .....Grandpa [Judge Henry] Brady

Carol's zippy grandmother from Kentucky blasts into town and Marcia and Jan think it would be great to fix her up with Mike's grandfather. They get him to the house with a ruse, and Grandma is playing basketball with the guys in the backyard. Grandpa Brady can't believe his eyes. They have a chat, but she's a little racy for him.

Marcia, Cindy, and Jan conspire with Alice to serve them a romantic, candlelit dinner. Mike and Carol are gone for the evening and the kids all disappear. The Judge thinks Connie planned it all. She gets furious and calls him an "old goat." He begs to remind her she's "no spring chicken." Alice is left holding a pan of flaming crêpes Suzette.

✿

The Judge is fond of quoting Latin and cites Pliny the Elder, a Roman scholar who lived from A.D. 23 to 79. His surviving work is an encyclopedia of natural history and he died trying to observe Vesuvius as it was erupting. The other scholar Judge Brady quotes is Marcus Seneca (54 B.C.–A.D. 39), a Spaniard who lived in Rome and who wrote a series of essays on the law.

94. "YOU CAN'T WIN 'EM ALL"
March 16, 1973
Written by Lois Hire
Directed by Jack Donahue
Regulars: Reed, Henderson, Davis, McCormick, Plumb, Olsen, Williams, Knight, Lookinland
Guests: Edward Knight as ....Monty Marshall
Vicki Schreck as ....Woodside Girl
Harlen Carraher as....................Clinton Boy
Claudio Martinez as ....Woodside Boy
Miyoshi Williams as ....Clinton Girl
Tracey M. Lee as..................Woodside Girl

Cindy's thrilled that she's in the running to be on a TV quiz show, *Question the Kids*. Bobby was selected too, but he seems oddly underwhelmed. Cindy studies and Bobby doesn't and she makes it and he doesn't. Cindy spends hours choosing her hairstyle and dress for her TV appearance. The trouble is, the night of the broadcast is the same night Mike and Carol have scheduled a huge smorgasbord for 26 friends and friends of friends—for which they've already bought the food.

By the night of the show, the rest of the kids are so fed up with Cindy's swelled head, they refuse to go with her. They do, however, want to watch the show—so they can see her fail.

✿

There have been a number of quiz shows for kids on TV over the years. The most famous were the long-running College Bowl and Quiz Kids, which both ran on Sunday afternoons.

When Mike suggests mortgaging the house to buy steaks for 14, he refers to the very high price of meat at the time.

95. "A ROOM AT THE TOP"
March 23, 1973
Written by William Raynor and Myles Wilder
Directed by Lloyd Schwartz
Regulars: Reed, Henderson, Davis, McCormick, Plumb, Olsen, Williams, Knight, Lookinland
Guest: Chris Beaumont as . . . . Hank [Carter]

Greg is dying for some privacy and when a pal who's already in college asks him to share his apartment, Greg wants to jump at the opportunity. But Mike says no. However, when the family clears out the attic for a charity drive, Greg asks Mike if he can have the attic for his room. Mike thinks it's a great idea.

Meanwhile, Marcia's in the same boat and she asks Carol if she can have the attic for her room and Carol agrees. When the two potential tenants arrive with their stuff, a territorial battle ensues. Mike and Carol discuss it and since Greg is a year older, he gets the room. Marcia's devastated.

❀

This title refers to the actual episode topic, but it does bring to mind the 1959 Laurence Harvey film Room at the Top, a critically acclaimed film which spawned a phrase, several sequels, and won Oscars for Harvey's costar Simone Signoret and the screenwriter, Neil Patterson. The title in that case was a little less literal.

The attic is obviously large enough to be made into two rooms—easy with an architect in the family—it's odd no one thinks to do it.

THE FIFTH SEASON

1973-1974

FRIDAY NIGHTS—FALL 1973

	ABC	CBS	NBC
8:00	THE BRADY BUNCH	Calucci's Department	Sanford and Son
8:30	The Odd Couple	Roll Out	The Girl with Something Extra
9:00	Room 222	CBS Friday Night Movie	Needles and Pins
9:30	Adam's Rib		The Brian Keith Show
10:00	Love, American Style		The Dean Martin Comedy Hour
10:30			

FRIDAY NIGHTS—WINTER 1973–74

	ABC	CBS	NBC
8:00	THE BRADY BUNCH	Dirty Sally	Sanford and Son
8:30	The Six Million Dollar Man	Good Times	Lotsa Luck
9:00		CBS Friday Night Movie	The Girl with Something Extra
9:30	The Odd Couple		The Brian Keith Show
10:00	Toma		The Dean Martin Comedy Hour
10:30			

SEASON RATINGS
October 1973–April 1974

1.	All in the Family	31.2
2.	The Waltons	28.1
3.	Sanford and Son	27.5
4.	M*A*S*H	25.7
5.	Hawaii Five-O	24.0
6.	Maude	23.5
7.	Kojak	23.3
	The Sonny and Cher Comedy Hour	23.3
9.	The Mary Tyler Moore Show	23.1
	Cannon	23.1
11.	The Six Million Dollar Man	22.7
12.	The Bob Newhart Show	22.3
	The Wonderful World of Disney	22.3
14.	NBC Sunday Mystery Movie	22.2
15.	Gunsmoke	22.1
16.	Happy Days	21.5
17.	Good Times	21.4
	Barnaby Jones	21.4
19.	ABC Monday Night Football	21.2
	CBS Friday Night Movie	21.2
21.	Tuesday Movie of the Week	21.0
22.	The Streets of San Francisco	20.8
23.	Adam 12	20.7
	ABC Sunday Night Movie	20.7
25.	The Rookies	20.3

THE WORLD
1973

- Former President Lyndon Baines Johnson died of a heart attack on January 22.
- Notable films of the year included *Save the Tiger*, *The Paper Chase*, *THX 1138*, *The Last Picture Show*, *Paper Moon*, *Bang the Drum Slowly*, and *The Exorcist*. Musicals included *Jesus Christ Superstar*, *Lost Horizon*, and *Godspell*. *The Godfather* and *Cabaret* swept the Oscars for the previous year's work.
- Members of the American Indian Movement occupied Wounded Knee on the Oglala Sioux reservation in South Dakota to protest American government treatment of American Indians, beginning a 70-day siege. A cease-fire was eventually worked out.
- War erupted on the Golan Heights on Yom Kippur between Syria, Egypt, and Israel. Following this, an Arab oil embargo cut the United States off from its main source of fuel supply, protesting the U.S. Middle East policy of supporting Israel.
- President Nixon signed a bill to build a trans-Alaska oil pipeline.
- The popular music idols of 1973 included Bette Midler, the Osmonds, the Jackson Five, David Cassidy, and British group Slade. British rocker David Essex became a star and a new variation of contemporary music emerged called "Philly Soul." Singer Jim Croce died in

an airplane crash shortly after leading the charts with "Bad, Bad Leroy Brown."

- In Vietnam, Americans were going home at last. The first group of American POWs released by Hanoi were flown to the U.S. in February, then North Vietnam threatened not to release any more POWs unless there was a cease-fire. Several days later, 12 nations at the Paris peace conference signed the Vietnam Settlement. In October, Nixon's negotiator, Henry Kissinger, and his North Vietnamese counterpart, Le Duc Tho, were awarded the Nobel Peace Prize.

- Pepsi-Cola became the first American product sold in the Soviet Union after a landmark agreement.

- Argentina held its first free elections since 1965, electing Peronista candidate Héctor J. Cámpora president, paving the way for the return of former dictator Juan Perón from exile in Madrid. He did return and was elected president in September. His third wife, Isabel, was his vice-president, the position so intensely desired by former wife Eva, before she died of cancer in 1954.

- Bestsellers of the year included Norman Mailer's biography of Monroe, *Marilyn*; Kurt Vonnegut's *Breakfast of Champions*; Graham Greene's *The Honorary Consul*, and Joseph Wambaugh's *The Onion Field*. J. R. R. Tolkien, author of The *Lord of the Rings* trilogy, died.

- Generalissimo Francisco Franco resigned as premier of Spain but retained the office of chief of state.

- Secretariat won thoroughbred racing's Triple Crown, the first horse to do so since 1948.

- Vice President Spiro Agnew resigned after he was indicted and pled no contest on income tax evasion charges. Gerald R. Ford took office as the 40th vice president in December.

TELEVISION
1973

- The event of the year was President Nixon's January 23 announcement on television that American involvement in Vietnam was ending.
- The biggest ruckus of the year was regarding the *All in the Family* spinoff, *Maude*, when it aired a program about abortion.
- CBS got 390,000 pieces of hate mail when it supposedly announced plans to air X-rated movies. It had made no such announcement, and had aired only one heavily censored, once-X-rated film—*The Damned*—on the late show, and planned no more.
- *The Six Million Dollar Man* (originally titled *Cyborg*) aired October 20, and *Kojak* (originally spelled *Cojack*) hit the streets of New York at the end of October.
- Other new series that fall included Monte Markham as *The New Perry Mason* (viewers preferred the old one), Sally Field as *The Girl with Something Extra* (she had psychic powers), Bill Bixby as *The Magician*, and Diana Rigg as a department store fashion coordinator.

    Crime shows were the rage that fall. *TV Guide* noted there would eventually be 29 of them on the air. NBC's *Wednesday Mystery Movie* added James McEachin as a black private eye on *Tenafly*, Mildred Natwick and Helen Hayes as *The Snoop Sisters*, and Dan Dailey did a turn as a detective on *Faraday and Company*. Jimmy Stewart mixed cornpone with the courtroom in *Hawkins*, and Richard Roundtree brought P. I. John Shaft from the big to the small screen—sans some of the violence and, er, permissiveness. *Police Story* and *Chase* (about an undercover cop unit in L.A.) rounded out the law-and-order gang.

The new sitcoms struggled and didn't make it: *Bob & Carol & Ted & Alice* was another big screen rip-off. *Needles and Pins* took us backstairs in Manhattan's rag trade, and *Lotsa Luck* didn't have much despite the presence of the comedic talents of Kathleen Freeman, Dom DeLuise, Wynn Irwin, Jack Knight, and Beverly Sanders. It was based on a British sitcom, a tactic which had worked so well with *All in the Family* and *Sanford and Son*.

The show with the most going for it was *Adam's Rib*, based on the wondrous film with Spencer Tracy and Katherine Hepburn as dueling married lawyers, but even the charming and quirky Blythe Danner and Ken Howard couldn't quite make it click.

- Tom Snyder premiered his late, late night show, *Tomorrow*.
- Departing from the TV landscape were the long-running *Mission: Impossible*, *The Mod Squad*, *Laugh-In*, *Search*, *Cool Million*, *Madigan*, and the variety shows of Bill Cosby, Doris Day, Julie Andrews, and Bobby Darin.
- Katharine Hepburn made her television debut in Tennessee Williams's *The Glass Menagerie*.
- Princess Anne's wedding was seen live by over 500 million people.
- The networks were all planning their bicentennial coverage. In fact, NBC had already started its *The American Experience* programming and CBS expected to begin a 13-part series, *The American Parade*, by 1974.
- There was daily satellite coverage of the Arab-Israeli War.
- The Nielsen rating service began its new "overnight" ratings in major markets with the fall '73 shows. NBC was behind the new service, but ABC refused to subscribe, saying it wanted "people ratings"—more demographic information about who's watching—rather than faster numbers for the homes with TV sets tuned to

particular shows. That season Nielsen only reported NBC and CBS shows in the overnights.

- ABC let Jack Paar go after an unsuccessful try by the long-time late-night host to regain his former ratings strength. It was reportedly considering Geraldo Rivera to replace Paar after the success of his special *Good Night, America,* a magazine-style show.
- Hope Lange wanted out of *The New Dick Van Dyke Show,* claiming her role as his wife had been "locked into pouring coffee and being an understanding house-keeper."
- Ozzie Nelson returned to TV this year in a syndicated sitcom called *Ozzie's Girls.*
- Harlan Ellison planned to launch his answer to *Star Trek* (*The Starlost*) as a syndicated series, and it was sold to NBC and Group W affiliates, but the writers' strike put it on indefinite hold.

THE BRADY BUNCH
1973

For the new season, Florence Henderson had her zillionth new hairstyle (and the best one yet). The biggest change is that the kids now seem to be young adults. Marcia gets her driver's license and her first job, Jan's more self-confident than in past seasons and also gets a job, and Peter's avidly seeking dates (and a job). Cindy finally loses her sausage ponytails.

Mike gets a new car (and about time), a red Chevy convertible, but the house is remarkably unchanged (thanks both to the chintzy Paramount budget and the same establishing shots that had been used since 1969. The girls' room is redecorated from baby pink to a more adult beige.

Suddenly six Brady kids weren't enough for the network. ABC felt that, since the kids were all so grown up, they needed to add a smaller child, oblivious to the fact that the show was popular not because it had small kids on it, but because everybody wanted to know what was going on with the six kids with whom they'd grown up. Yet near the end of the season, Carol Brady's heretofore unmentioned nephew Oliver appeared.

And the show was still stuck opposite the number three show on the air, *Sanford and Son*. Not that the shows necessarily had the same audience, but they were both comedies, and *Sanford* probably did siphon off some potential *Brady* watchers. And so CBS, in its infinite wisdom, put a new show opposite these two comedy hits and it was, what else? A comedy. *Calcucci's Department* starred James Coco as head of a New York unemployment office. Mr. Coco and the cast were unemployed by December.

ABC moved *The Partridge Family* to Saturday nights, but the block following the Bradys was still all comedy, with the addition of the superb *Adam's Rib,* taken from a classic Katharine Hepburn-Spencer Tracy film about a married defense attorney and prosecutor. It starred Blythe Danner and Ken Howard, but this sophisticated comedy was also gone by December.

In December, ABC changed the entire look of its Friday night lineup. The Bradys were now isolated, followed by a heavily dramatic action show, *The Six Million Dollar Man*, then back to comedy with *The Odd Couple*, then even heavier drama with *Toma*, an intense police drama starring Tony Musante and Simon Oakland.

If you wonder why the only two comedies weren't together, there was a trend at the time to start one-hour dramas on the half-hour, thus (hopefully) preventing audiences from switching on the hour to a program starting on another network.

All these machinations knocked even *The Partridge Family* out of the top shows, but *The Six Million Dollar Man* was just a hair out of the top ten (Friday nights are traditionally good nights for science fiction).

No one knew this would be the last season for *The Brady Bunch*.

THE EPISODES

96. "ADIOS, JOHNNY BRAVO"
September 14, 1973
Written by Joanna Lee
Directed by Jerry London
Regulars: Reed, Henderson, Davis, McCormick, Plumb, Olsen, Williams, Knight, Lookinland
Guests: Claudia Jennings as .... Tami Cutler
Paul Cavonis as .... Buddy Berkman
Jeff David as.......................... Hal Barton
Songs: "You've Got To Be In Love (To Love a Love Song)"
"Good Time Music" .... Barry Williams and the Brady Kids
"Heading To the Mountains" .... Barry Williams

The kids audition for the Hal Barton Talent Show and win a spot on the next week's show. In the audience is talent agent Tami Cutler and she finds Greg and announces his profile would "look great on an album cover." She asks him to call her the next day. The kids all think she's interested in them as a group, but it's only Greg she's after.

He goes to her office [a psychedelic wonder!] and meets her partner, who asks him to play the electric guitar. They like his playing. Soon, Tami has Greg in a glitzy costume. They tell him he's the new Johnny Bravo. He's flattered, but a bit worried that they don't want the rest of the family. But that's nothing compared to the kids' reaction to the news. Marcia thinks he sold out and Cindy calls him a "small person."

Mike and Carol are dubious about the whole thing, and are really upset when Greg decides not to go to college.

❁

We learn that Carol went to State University and Mike went to Norton College.

There are a number of Brady Kids recordings, but the songs from this episode were never recorded. This story was one used in 1995's The Brady Bunch Movie, *but Greg was given a new song.*

Andrew J. Edelstein and Frank Lovece, in The Brady Bunch Book, *tell the interesting and tragic story of Claudia Jennings. She was a* Playboy *Playmate, starred in a number of cheesy "B" movies, and died in 1979 in a car accident.*

Paul Cavonis guested on Rhoda *and in a Don Johnson TV movie,* The City. *Jeff David was the voice of Crichton the Robot in 1981's* Buck Rogers in the 25th Century.

Joanna Lee wrote for Sherwood Schwartz's Gilligan's Island *and now produces and writes afterschool specials for young people. She also wrote the TV movies* Mary Jane Harper Cried Last Night *and* The Waltons Thanksgiving Special.

97. "MAIL ORDER HERO"
September 21, 1973
Written by Martin Ragaway
Directed by Bruce Bilson
Regulars: Reed, Henderson, Davis, McCormick, Plumb, Olsen, Williams, Knight, Lookinland
Guests: Joe Namath ....[Himself]
       Tim Herbert as ....Herb [Keller]
       Kerry MacLane as.................... Eric [Parker]
       Eric Woods as.................................Tom
       Larry Michaels as .... Burt

Bobby dreams of playing football with Joe Namath. In fact, the dream's so real, the next day, he brags to his friends that he knows the New York Jets superstar personally. Mike and Carol take pity on Bobby and try to think of someone they know who might know Namath, but there's no one.

Then when she hears about another star who went 1,200 miles out of his way to visit a sick child, Cindy writes a letter to Namath about his grievous illness, signing Bobby's name.

✿

Joe Namath was a big deal at the time, being part super-jock, part cover boy, and part TV star. He seemed to be everywhere doing advertisements, and even endorsed a line of pantyhose in TV commercials.

When Marcia reads about Mike Connors visiting a sick child, it's a bit of an inside joke, since Robert Reed also costarred on Mike Connors' TV show, Mannix.

Howard Cosell was a controversial, erudite, and long-winded sports commentator.

The outtakes from Bobby's dream were aired for the first time in Susan Olsen's 1995 TV special, The Brady Bunch Home Movies.

98. "SNOW WHITE AND THE SEVEN BRADYS"
September 28, 1973
Written by Ben Starr
Directed by Bruce Bilson
Regulars: Reed, Henderson, Davis, McCormick, Plumb, Olsen, Williams, Knight, Lookinland
Guests: Allan Melvin .... Sam
Elvenn Havard as .... Policeman
Frances Whitfield as .... School Teacher

Cindy's beloved teacher Mrs. Whitfield is retiring and the class wants to buy her a set of books she likes, but they cost $200. Cindy suggests they do a play, *Snow White and the Seven Dwarfs*. Everybody loves the idea, then Cindy volunteers her whole family to play all the parts.

Convincing the participants isn't the easiest job in the world, but finally everyone agrees. The rest of the class takes care of programs, advertising, and printing the tickets. Cindy is in charge of booking the theater, but she goofs up and it's rented. Cindy's sure she's ruined the whole thing.

❀

Ever see a market with all-black tarpaper windows? There once was one on the Paramount lot—while they were shooting this episode. There's also no mention of who wrote the tongue-in-cheek version of Snow White *that the Bradys perform, though it was probably the author of the episode, Ben Starr.*

99. "NEVER TOO YOUNG"
October 5, 1973
Written by Al Schwartz and Larry Rhine
Directed by Richard Michaels
Regulars: Reed, Henderson, Davis, McCormick, Plumb, Olsen, Williams, Knight, Lookinland
Guests: Melissa Anderson as .... Millicent
Song: "I Wanna Be Loved by You" .... Mike and Carol

Bobby gets his first kiss from a girl when Millicent comes over to thank him for helping her at school. Faster than he can say "Yech," he sees fireworks. Then he gets worried that somebody will find out. He doesn't realize Cindy is watching.

Bobby starts to wonder if he imagined the skyrockets and goes over to Millicent's house and kisses her again to see what happens. History repeats itself. But Millicent tells him he shouldn't have done that. She may have the mumps.

❀

When Bobby dreams of Millicent running toward him in slow motion Schwartz was parodying a Miss Clairol commercial of that time. The skyrockets Bobby sees may be a classic device, but it was also used several times every week in Love, American Style, *that ran from 1969 to 1974.*

The full view of the exterior used for Millicent's house is the one used as Carol Tyler Miller's house in the wedding pilot. However, it doesn't match the close-up house exterior (yellow and white clapboard) in color, style or physical lay-out.

"I Wanna Be Loved by You" was the song that made "boop-boop-a-doop" girl Helen Kane famous. The song was written in 1928 for her first musical on Broadway, Good Boy. *Debbie Reynolds played Helen Kane in the film* Three Little Words, *but when she sang the song, Kane herself dubbed the song on the soundtrack. But by far the most famous rendition is Marilyn Monroe's in the 1959 film* Some Like it Hot.

When Jan mentions the medical prowess of Marcus Welby, she refers to the Robert Young TV show Marcus Welby, M.D., *which ran from 1969 to 1976.*

100. "PETER AND THE WOLF"
October 12, 1973
Written by Tam Spiva
Directed by Leslie H. Martinson

Regulars: Reed, Henderson, Davis, McCormick, Plumb, Olsen, Williams, Knight, Lookinland

Guests: Cindi Crosby as .... Sandra
Paul Fierro as .... Mr. [Juan] Calderon
Alma Beltran as .... Mrs. [Maria] Calderon
Bill Miller as .... Len
Kathie Gibboney as .... Linda

Greg's got a date with the hottest girl in school, and every guy in his class is green with envy. But then Sandra tells him she has to break her date because her cousin Linda's coming to town. Greg finds out that Linda's 18 and he offers to find a date for her, and Sandra thinks it's a great idea. She hasn't seen Linda in six years, but Greg assumes she looks like Sandra. His friends assume she looks like Frankenstein.

Meanwhile, the Bradys brush up on their Spanish (and Alice brushes up on her enchiladas) to entertain some clients from Mexico. Greg finally coerces Peter (with fake moustache) into being Linda's date. Linda is a knockout.

At the drive-in, Peter's a nervous wreck, and eats his fake moustache along with the popcorn. Later, Linda and Sandra figure out what the guys are doing, and they decide to get back at them.

❀

Note that the movie Greg, Peter, Linda, and Sandra attend is the same film he and Rachel watched in episode #87, "Greg Gets Grounded" (and the same drive-in theater).

Susan Olsen says, "My favorite episode is the one where Greg and Peter go on a double date because I think it has some of the funniest material that was ever on The Brady Bunch."

101. "GETTING GREG'S GOAT"
October 19, 1973
Written by Milton Pascal &* Sam Locke
Directed by Robert Reed
Regulars: Reed, Henderson, Davis, McCormick, Plumb, Olsen, Williams, Knight, Lookinland
Guests: George D. Wallace as .... Mr. Binkley
Sandra Gould as .... Mrs. Gould
Margarita Cordova as .... First PTA Lady
Selma Archerd as ....Second PTA Lady

Greg sneaks in late one night with Raquel. No, the eldest Brady kid hasn't given in to his hormones. Raquel is the Coolidge High School mascot, and also a goat. The Westdale bear cub mascot was stolen before the big game between the rival schools, and he and some friends retaliated by taking Raquel.

Greg sneaks her up to his attic, but in the morning he finds that she's eaten his American history report. At breakfast, Mike reads about the pranks in the paper and tells Greg that when he was younger *he* stole his school rival's mascot and was suspended for a week. Alice and Mike discover you can hear everything said in the attic through the laundry closet air vent, and Mike thinks Greg's got a woman in his room. Then Carol joins a group of PTA mothers who think this mascot-stealing has to stop and plan severe punishment for the culprits.

✿

Sandra Gould also was long-time incredulous neighbor Gladys Kravitz on Bewitched. *She appeared in many, many television shows and also on* Gilligan's Island.

*Note that many of the writers are listed this season with an ampersand instead of the word "and." The Writers Guild, the union for TV and screenwriters, clarified credits and from this year forward, partners would use the ampersand, and when you see "and" separating names, it means that the different writers worked sequentially, not together, on the script.

Selma Archerd also plays a Brady neighbor in 1995's The Brady Bunch Movie.

102. "MARCIA GETS CREAMED"
November 26, 1973
Written by Ben Gershman and Bill Freedman
Directed by Peter Baldwin
Regulars: Reed, Henderson, Davis, McCormick, Plumb, Olsen, Williams, Knight, Lookinland
Guests: Henry Corden .... [Mr. Haskell]
Michael Gray as .... Jeff
Kimberly Beck as .... Girl

Peter's been looking for work all week and is irritated when Marcia lucks out and gets a job at Haskell's Ice Cream. The kids are thrilled, but poor Mike and Alice are on a diet. Marcia sees that Mr. Haskell is working too hard and suggests he take some time off. He asks where he's going to get another assistant as good as Marcia. She suggests Peter, and Mr. Haskell agrees and puts Marcia in charge of the afternoon shift.

But Peter goofs off, makes endless phone calls, refuses to work, and Marcia fires him. In addition, Marcia's job is cutting into her social life, so she suggests Jan for the job. And she's dynamite. Then Marcia's boyfriend Jeff comes into the shop with another girl. Mr. Haskell discovers his semi-retirement doesn't agree with him, so he's coming back to work afternoons and has to let one of the girls go. Jan's the better worker, so he fires Marcia.

❀

Henry Corden is not only the current voice of Fred Flintstone, he also appeared in a godawful flick, Blood Feast. *Corden also guest-starred in a wide variety of sitcoms, including* Rhoda, The Mary Tyler Moore Show, Family Affair, McHale's Navy, Bewitched, Camp Runamuck, Hennessey, It's About Time, The Monkees, *and* My Favorite Martian.

103. "MY BROTHER'S KEEPER"
November 2, 1973
Written by Michael Morris
Directed by Ross Bowman
Regulars: Reed, Henderson, Davis, McCormick, Plumb, Olsen, Williams, Knight, Lookinland

The guys are doing their chores: Greg's painting the shutters (green) on a ladder; Peter's working in the flower beds, and Bobby's on trash detail. Greg gets a phone call, and goes inside. Peter reaches for the hose, but it's tangled around the ladder—and a bucket of green paint—and both are headed for Peter's head. Bobby sees what's happening and pushes Peter out of the way, getting covered by green paint in the process. Peter tells Bobby he owes him his life and he'll be his slave forever.

Bobby says that's not necessary, but Peter does all Bobby's chores, builds him a Go-Kart, shines his shoes, oils his bike, cleans his closet, etc. It isn't long before Bobby realizes he's got a good thing going and takes advantage of Peter. Peter starts to resent the chores, and they're ruining his social life. His girlfriend stops speaking to him. Pretty soon, Peter and Bobby aren't speaking to each other.

❁

When Alice, commenting on the war between Bobby and Peter, says, "All's quiet on the western front," she quotes the title of one of the most famous antiwar novels ever, All Quiet on the Western Front, *a 1929 treatise by Erich Maria Remarque, a German journalist and novelist. He was deeply affected by the horrors of World War I, and fled Germany for America in 1932 to escape the Nazis. The story was filmed twice, in 1930 and 1979. The first version starred Lew Ayres, whose performance won an Oscar as did the picture and its director. The 1979 remake starred Richard Thomas, Ernest Borgnine and Patricia Neal and was a critical success.*

104. "QUARTERBACK SNEAK"
November 9, 1973
Written by Ben Gershman & Bill Freedman
Directed by Peter Baldwin
Regulars: Reed, Henderson, Davis, McCormick, Plumb, Olsen, Williams, Knight, Lookinland
Guests: Denny Miller as . . . . Tank Gates
Chris Beaumont as . . . . Jerry Rogers
Don Carter as . . . . Rich

The big game is Saturday, Westdale vs. Fairview. The Fairview High quarterback, Jerry Rogers, makes a pass at Marcia as she puts up "Beat Fairview" posters. She's surprised, but he's a hunk. She doesn't know it's part of a larger plan to get at Greg (who's halfback on the Westdale team). Greg tells her she's a traitor.

Meanwhile, Carol hears from Tank Gates, a football hero from her own Westdale senior year. In fact, they "went together," and Mike gets a little jealous.

Jerry drives Marcia home after school and while she's not looking, he tries to steal Greg's playbook. But Bobby sees him and tells Greg. Marcia insists Jerry didn't do it, but Greg plans to test him by making a fake and putting Jerry and temptation together.

✿

Denny Miller, who plays Fairview quarterback Jerry Rogers, starred as the surfer who ends up on Gilligan's Island *in "Big Man on a Little Stick" in the first season of the show. He's also married to Kit Smythe, the actress who played Ginger in the original* Gilligan's Island *pilot. Today he produces fitness videotapes.*

When Jerry tells Marcia she's got eyes like Faye Dunaway, he refers to the versatile actress who, in 1973, appeared in Oklahoma Crude. *In 1974, she would appear in one of her most famous films,* Chinatown.

105. "TRY, TRY AGAIN"
November 16, 1973
Written by Al Schwartz & Larry Rhine
Directed by George Tyne
Regulars: Reed, Henderson, Davis, McCormick, Plumb, Olsen, Williams, Knight, Lookinland
Guests: Judy Landon as...................... Miss Clairette
Ruth Anson as..................... Mrs. Ferguson
Darryl Seman as ....Billy Naylor

When Jan is eliminated from her ballet class's recital, she quits the class in despair. She really wanted to dance. Carol suggests there are other kinds of dancing, so Jan tries tap, but she's no good at that either, and the rest of the family is going berserk with the noise. Carol and Marcia agree Jan just has to find the thing at which she's good.

Marcia teaches her to be a drum majorette, but she's a klutz with the baton. Jan's positive she'll never be good at anything. The kids all try to buck up her self-confidence—Greg lets her win at Ping-Pong, Cindy and Marcia let her wipe them out at Monopoly, and Peter and Bobby let her win at darts. But Mike and Carol think it's a lousy idea.

❀

When Alice jokingly compares herself to Raquel Welch, she's referring to the statuesque beauty who made a splash with the 1966 "B" films One Million Years B.C. *and* Fantastic Voyage. *In 1971, she gained a lot of credibility with her performance in* Kansas City Bomber, *but she was still known for her incredible body. Welch is an intelligent and versatile actress, and she added singing and dancing to her repertoire later in her career by taking over for Lauren Bacall in the hit Broadway musical* Woman of the Year. *When Alice mentions Shirley Temple, she is of course referring to the most famous child star of them all, who tap danced in many of her films, often in the company of the grand-master of tap, Bill "Bojangles" Robinson.*

106. "THE CINCINNATI KIDS"
November 23, 1973
Written by Al Schwartz & Larry Rhine
Directed by Leslie H. Martinson
Regulars: Reed, Henderson, Davis, McCormick, Plumb, Olsen, Williams, Knight, Lookinland
Guests: Hilary Thompson .... [Marge]
          Bob Hoffman as........................... Attendant
          L. Jeffrey Schwartz as .... The Bear/Man

Mike's got another surprise for the family. He's been doing work for a big Cincinnati amusement park, and he's taking the whole family to the park while he meets with the owners. Mike's meeting is in the afternoon, so the family goes on all the rides, including a very hairy roller-coaster. Greg even manages to make time with a pretty park employee, Marge.

Mike joins them for a bit, and Jan asks him to store a poster she bought in one of his cylinders containing his plans for the meeting. The cylinders get switched and then Jan loses the one with the plans in it. Mike ends up at the meeting with a Yogi Bear poster and his clients are leaving on a plane for New York in half an hour.

❀

This episode was shot at King's Island Amusement Park. It looks like it has some great rides.

The L. Jeffrey Schwartz credited as the man in the bear suit is, of course, series producer (and son of Sherwood) Lloyd Schwartz.

107. "THE ELOPEMENT"
December 7, 1973
Written by Harry Winkler
Directed by Jerry London
Regulars: Reed, Henderson, Davis, McCormick, Plumb, Olsen, Williams, Knight, Lookinland
Guests: Allan Melvin as .... Sam

Byron Webster as .... The Reverend
Bella Bruck as .... Gladys [Harris]

Sam's cousin Clara is secretly eloping, and she wants Sam and Alice to stand up for her. Marcia and Jan come in as she's talking to Sam about it, and they're sure that Alice is talking about eloping with Sam next Sunday—after Sam and Alice's bowling tournament. Everybody in the family tries their best to pry the "secret" out of Alice and Sam, but since they don't know what everybody's talking about, they don't comply.

Alice thinks the whole family's going nuts, the way everybody keeps giggling when she walks in the room. When she asks for Saturday night off for the bowling tournament, everyone thinks that's when the wedding is to be and they start planning a surprise reception. Carol calls an agency to get a replacement for Alice while she's on her honeymoon, and when she's interviewing, Alice overhears the conversation and concludes they're firing her. *Then*, she and Sam have a fight.

❀

Recently, Ann B. Davis reflected on the popularity of the show. She feels it only really became a bona fide hit after its initial run. "When we went into syndication, we were the only decent show to play at 3:30 after the kids got home from school, and suddenly there were 60 channels available and no software, so we fell into that."

108. "MISS POPULARITY"
December 21, 1973
Written by Martin Ragaway
Directed by Jack Donohue
Regulars: Reed, Henderson, Davis, McCormick, Plumb, Olsen, Williams, Knight, Lookinland
Guests: Darryl Seman as .... Herman
Jerelyn Fields as .... Shirley

Jan's up for Most Popular Girl at school, and she's thrilled. And terrified. She thinks she's not "beautiful, brainy, and built," like her competitor Kathy Williams. The whole family pitches in to help her win. Alice even bakes fortune cookies with Jan's name on the fortunes.

Jan promises to do favors for everyone who votes for her, including algebra tutoring and babysitting. Jan wins, and her constituents start calling in the favors. Greg doesn't have time to tutor Herman in algebra and Jan doesn't have time to babysit Shirley's brother. In fact, a whole lot of the kids are mad that Jan refuses to honor her promises, even to her sisters and brothers. She even louses up a getaway weekend Carol and Mike have counted on for ages.

✿

Barry Williams thinks he knows why the actors who played the Bradys didn't get swelled heads as Jan does in this episode: "I think that what saved us on The Brady Bunch, is that we had each other to relate to and to talk to. When you're going through an unusual experience, if you've got people that are going through it with you, it's a lot easier."

109. "KELLY'S KIDS"
January 4, 1974
Written and created by Sherwood Schwartz
Directed by Richard Michaels
Regulars: Reed, Henderson, Davis, McCormick, Plumb, Olsen, Williams, Knight, Lookinland
Guests:

Ken Berry	[Ken Kelly]
Brooke Bundy	[Kathy Kelly]
Todd Lookinland as	Matt
William Attmore II as	Dwayne
Carey Wong as	Steve
Jackie Joseph as	Miss Phillips
Molly Dodd as	Mrs. Payne

Kathy and Ken Kelly surprise Mike and Carol with the news that they've adopted a son. After Matt's first day in their home, the Kellys decide Matt misses his friends from the orphanage and they decide to adopt another boy so he has a companion. But Matt has two best friends at the orphanage, one black and one Asian. They decide to adopt both boys.

So the Kellys, Matt, Dwayne, and Carey start to forge life as a family. The first battle is over the beds in the boys' room. Carey and Dwayne challenge Matt's right to the best bed, and a pillow fight erupts.

❀

Ah, here you see a television institution—take a pilot for a new show, bookend it with established series characters and voilà! New show—hopefully a hit. The Brady Bunch had just about run its course, and for Sherwood Schwartz it was time to think about the next project. But this time, it didn't work and it's not hard to see why. Take three parts Brady *(including Mike Lookinland's brother), add one part* Bewitched *(the interfering neighbor), one part* Dick Van Dyke *(Kelly's show biz job), and you end up with . . . mashed potatoes. Amazingly, though this idea was a little dated even in 1974, 12 years later, CBS dusted it off and premiered it in 1986 as a new show,* Together We Stand.

Note that the Kellys' house bears a remarkable resemblance to the Bradys'. The furniture's been switched around a little, and the wallpaper's different, but not much else.

Ken Berry may be best known for his indelible comedy shows Mayberry R.F.D. *and* F Troop, *but he's really a song-and-dance man and was very much in demand to appear on all the variety shows in the '60s and '70s.*

110. "THE DRIVER'S SEAT"
January 11, 1974
Written by George Tibbles
Directed by Jack Arnold

Regulars: Reed, Henderson, Davis, McCormick, Plumb, Olsen, Williams, Knight, Lookinland
Guest: Herb Vigran as ....Examiner

Marcia gets the highest score in her driver's ed. class, but she gets no respect at home. Greg's derisive about women drivers. He bets Marcia six whole months of chores that she won't pass her driver's test on the first try. But success isn't running in the Brady family this week—Jan's debating team goes down in defeat and she says she's the reason they lost. Marcia gives Jan a real pep talk about psyching herself up for the next debate.

No one—least of all Marcia—thinks she lacks any confidence, but she fails, absolutely freezing on her driving test and embarrassing herself completely.

❁

The driving contest is held on the Paramount lot. As Mission: Impossible *proved, there were unlimited things you could do on the backlot. Many sitcoms didn't do much exterior shooting, but* The Brady Bunch *seems less claustrophobic than other shows because it did do a lot of backlot shooting, in addition to going on location for the season openers.*

111. "OUT OF THIS WORLD"
January 18, 1974
Written by Al Schwartz & Larry Rhine
Directed by Peter Baldwin
Regulars: Reed, Henderson, Davis, McCormick, Plumb, Olsen, Williams, Knight, Lookinland
Guests: Brigadier General James A. McDivitt ....[Himself]
       Mario Machado ....[Himself]
       James Flavin................. [Captain McCaffney]
       Frank and Sadie Delfino as ....The Kaplutians

Bobby and Peter go to a TV studio to see an interview with astronaut Jim McDivitt, who says that during the flight of

Gemini IV they saw a UFO. He thinks it's super-egotistical for us to think we're the only life in the universe. Later, Peter and Bobby ask for autographs and ask General McDivitt if he saw anyone in the UFO (he didn't).

That night, Peter and Bobby are awakened by a strange noise and lights. They rush to the window and see a UFO. The next day, none of their friends at school believe them. They come home and ask Carol if they can camp out tonight in the backyard and borrow her camera to get some proof. They see it again, and photograph it. Upstairs, Marcia comes into Greg's attic and catches him in the act. He's using a masked flashlight and whistle to simulate the UFO.

❀

Frank and Sadie Delfino, who play the Kaplutians, were the stand-ins for Eve, Mike, Chris, and Susan during all the years of the show. They also occasionally appeared in crowd scenes.

Barry's lower lip is bandaged because this episode was shot just after he had a serious auto accident and had stitches from splitting his lip on the steering wheel.

Mario Machado is a real Los Angeles newscaster. He's worked for CBS, PBS, and various radio stations. He's made quite a career out of playing newsmen in TV and movies, and has appeared in Blue Thunder, St. Elmo's Fire, RoboCop I *and* III, *and lots of TV shows, including a 1995–96 episode of* Murder, She Wrote.

112. "WELCOME ABOARD"
January 24, 1974
Written by Larry Rhine & Al Schwartz
Directed by Richard Michaels
Regulars: Reed, Henderson, Davis, McCormick, Plumb, Olsen, Williams, Knight, Lookinland
Guests: John Nolan as........................ Mr. Douglas
Judd Laurance as..........................Director

Robbie Rist as .... Oliver
Snag Werris as .... Keystone Cop
Dick Winslow as .... Truck Driver #1
Ralph Montgomery as .... Truck Driver #2

When Carol announces to Mike they're going to have an addition to the family, Cindy and Bobby overhear. The whole family then thinks Carol's pregnant, until she straightens them out. Her nephew Oliver is coming to live with them for a while. The kids are excited until they discover Oliver is a jinx. He seems to carry disaster around with him.

The bunks go back in Bobby and Peter's room. Oliver turns out to be a world-class snorer. The kids discuss the problem and, unfortunately, Oliver overhears. Later, Carol finds him in Tiger's doghouse. Mike has a talk with him and the other kids and they all make a big effort, then with one toss of a basketball, Oliver destroys Marcia's hand-painted ceramic pot (a school assignment) and a building model Mike says took him almost as long to make as a real building.

✿

Oliver escapes to the doghouse after all his disasters, even though Tiger was long gone. Susan Olsen says, "We kept the doghouse long after Tiger was gone because our lawn was Astroturf and one day a light fell on the lawn and created a big, melted, molten Astroturf area, so we kept the doghouse."

When the family visits a movie studio, that studio is, of course, Paramount. They enter through the fabled Bronson Gate (seen in a zillion films, including Billy Wilder's Sunset Boulevard*) and the studio is called Marathon Studios. The original address of Paramount was on Marathon, a street eventually absorbed by studio expansion (as was the Bronson Gate).*

113. "TWO PETES IN A POD"
February 8, 1974
Written by Sam Locke & Milton Pascal
Directed by Richard Michaels
Regulars: Reed, Henderson, Davis, McCormick, Plumb, Olsen, Williams, Knight, Lookinland
Guests: Christopher Knight as . . . . Arthur [Owens]
　　　　　Robbie Rist as . . . . Oliver
　　　　　Denise Nickerson as . . . . Pamela [Phillips]
　　　　　Kathy O'Dare as . . . . Michelle

Peter's finally gotten a date with a girl, Michelle, who he's been chasing all semester. Then he's astonished to discover he has a double at school, Arthur Owens, a new kid. Pete suggests Arthur come home with him to fake out his family. They get to the house, and Arthur removes his glasses and the deception works great.

Mike gets a call from Mr. Phillips, who asks Arthur to entertain his niece visiting from out of town on Friday night. When the real Peter takes over again, he realizes he's got a conflict. He's taking Michelle to a costume party, and Mike insists he honor Arthur's commitment to entertain Pamela, Mr. Phillips' niece. Peter calls Arthur and arranges for him to handle the Pamela engagement. But it all comes flying apart when Arthur's late and Peter is forced into a farce of quick changes, swinging doors, and crossed signals.

✿

The music played for Peter's quick changes is "The William Tell Overture," long the theme song of another TV show, The Lone Ranger, *which ran on ABC from 1949 to 1957, starring Clayton Moore and Jay Silverheels. Silverheels guest-starred in two episodes of* The Brady Bunch *when he played Chief Dan Eagle Cloud in "Grand Canyon or Bust" and "The Brady Braves" at the beginning of the third season.*

114. "TOP SECRET"
February 15, 1973
Written by Howard Ostroff
Directed by Bernard Wiesen
Regulars: Reed, Henderson, Davis, McCormick, Plumb, Olsen, Williams, Knight, Lookinland
Guests: Allan Melvin .... Sam
Lew Palter as .... Mr. Gronsky
Don Fenwick as...................... Fred Sanders
Robbie Rist as .... Oliver

After five years of togetherness, it's a mystery why anybody still tries to keep a secret in the Brady clan with all their fertile minds happily leaping to conclusions. Mike's investigated by the FBI because he's working on a government project. Then Sam has a mysterious meeting with Mike, which he refuses to discuss with Alice.

The Brady women jump to the conclusion that Sam is building Alice their dream house and the marriage proposal will soon follow.

The younger Brady men deduce that Sam is a double agent, out to steal the plans Mike is working on.

❀

Robbie Rist, who plays Carol's nephew Oliver in the last few episodes, went on to play Ted Baxter's adopted son on The Mary Tyler Moore Show *and he was a regular on* Lucas Tanner *and* Battlestar Galactica. *Susan Olsen says, "I keep in touch with Robbie Rist somewhat and he's a musician. He's in a band called Wonder Boy and doing quite well."*

115. "THE SNOOPERSTAR"
February 22, 1974
Written by Harry Winkler
Directed by Bruce Bilson
Regulars: Reed, Henderson, Davis, McCormick, Plumb, Olsen, Williams, Knight, Lookinland

Guests: Natalie Schafer................[Penelope Fletcher]
            Robbie Rist as...............................Oliver
Song: ''On the Good Ship Lollipop'' .... Susan Olsen
                         and Natalie Schafer

Cindy's paranoid. She thinks her siblings are talking about her and are all in on some secret to which she isn't privy. Cindy enlists Oliver's help to find out what's going on. The first order of business is to read Marcia's diary. But Marcia catches on and intentionally puts in stuff to drive Cindy nuts.

They concoct a plan to convince Cindy a movie studio is seeking a new Shirley Temple—one of Cindy's obsessions—and that the talent scout is coming over to the house tonight. The only person who is coming to the Brady house is Mike's wealthy, eccentric, picky, and snobby client, Mrs. Penelope Fletcher, who is utterly bewildered when Cindy—replete with ringlets, Mary Janes, and a zillion petticoats—comes prancing down the stairs.

✿

The bane of Susan Olsen's existence was that Cindy was always doing dumb things she thought were juvenile. In this episode, she suffers the ultimate indignity—dressing up like Shirley Temple. She says her bit in this episode "would have been cute had I been seven, but I was twelve and quite awkward."

Nobody played a wealthy snob better than the irrepressible Natalie Schafer, forever identified with her role as Lovey Howell on Gilligan's Island. *Her line about usually dealing with the head of the firm, Mr. Matthews, is perfect, since he will be portrayed in the next episode by the man who played Lovey's husband, Thurston Howell III, Jim Backus.*

"On the Good Ship Lollipop" was written by Sidney Clare and Richard A. Whiting, and performed by Shirley Temple in her 1934 film Bright Eyes.

Why do Jan and Marcia need to go through the boy's room to gain access to their community bathroom to spy on Cindy? Is the door to the hall broken?

116. "THE HUSTLER"
March 1, 1974
Written by Bill Freedman & Ben Gershman
Directed by Michael J. Kane
Regulars: Reed, Henderson, Davis, McCormick, Plumb, Olsen, Williams, Knight, Lookinland
Guests: Jim Backus as .... Harry Matthews
Robbie Rist as .... Oliver
Dorothy Shay as .... Frances Matthews
Charles Stewart as..................... Joe Sinclair
Leonard Bremen as .... Truck Driver
Jason Dunn as.................... Hank Thompson
Susan Quick as.................. Gloria Thompson
Grayce Spence as.................. Muriel Sinclair

A truckload of crates arrives at the Brady house addressed to Mike and when they open them they find a pool table. Mike's in the dark as who sent it until the next morning, when he learns it was the head of his firm, Mr. Matthews, who's a pool freak.

Bobby turns out to be a natural pool player, and dreams of giving demonstrations of his prowess in front of the crowned heads of Europe.

Mike plans a dinner of appreciation for Matthews, which turns into a large gathering. The men adjourn to the garage (where the table is set up). The men manage to let Matthews win each game, until Bobby joins them and challenges him to a game. The boss doesn't enjoy the game so much when he's losing.

❀

The title refers to the classic 1961 movie about pool, The Hustler, *which starred Paul Newman as Fast Eddie, a two-bit pool hustler who ends up taking on the great Minnesota*

Fats. Jim Backus created many memorable characters, including the charming Mr. Magoo (sadly, it's now politically incorrect to make fun of visually-impaired people and the cartoons are seldom seen) and the man with more money than God, Thurston Howell III, on Gilligan's Island. Howell was actually based upon a character Backus used to do at parties, Hubert Updyke III. It was his wife, Henny, who urged him to use the character on a '40s radio show, and he revitalized him for the '60s sitcom.

117. "THE HAIR-BRAINED SCHEME"
March 8, 1974
Written by Chuck Stewart, Jr.
Directed by Jack Arnold
Regulars: Reed, Henderson, Davis, McCormick, Plumb, Olsen, Williams, Knight, Lookinland
Guests: John Wheeler as .... Second Man
Ben Hoffman as .... Man
Brandy Carson as .... Woman
Hope Sherwood as .... Gretchen
Barbara Bernstein as .... Suzanne
Robbie Rist as .... Oliver

All the kids are bitten by the entrepreneurial bug. Bobby starts selling a miracle hair tonic and Cindy decides to raise rabbits. Bobby receives a case of his stuff, and Cindy gets bunnies called Romeo and Juliet. Both enlist Oliver to assist them.

Bobby's door-to-door efforts are a complete failure. Greg takes pity on him and buys a bottle. Bobby administers the treatment personally, and it turns Greg's hair orange. Greg's graduation is the next day and he's ready to kill Bobby. To make things worse, when Carol tries to sneak Greg into her beauty parlor to have the damage repaired, he runs into two girls from school.

✿

In his book, Barry Williams says Robert Reed thought this script was so ridiculous that he refused to appear in it. This necessitates the completely unbelievable situation that Dad Brady would miss Greg's high school graduation for any reason. It also means that Reed doesn't appear in the show's final episode.

LOVE AND LUST ON THE BRADY SET

Because there were all those teenaged hormones on the set, the second most-asked question about *The Brady Bunch* is whether the kids dated each other.

Barry Williams has the answer. "We all teamed up at one time or another. Bobby and Cindy started it all off with a 7-year-old wedding ceremony—a mock wedding ceremony. Marcia and Jan presided over it and they used a lot of silly jokes in it, like 'wedded in holy macaroni' and 'awfully wedded bliss' and then Bobby grabbed Cindy and they ran off onto the set to find the only private spot on the set, Tiger's doghouse."

Susan Olsen picks up the story. "We had the wedding and then he decided he liked Eve better because she was developing and so we got divorced. The way we got a divorce was we did the marriage ceremony backwards. We walked backwards and instead of kissing each other, we kind of spat at each other and then we were divorced."

"It sounds strange that we dated one another, but as we grew up, we were who we knew the best," says Barry Williams. "And we were around each other more than our own families. We were always pushed together for those tight shots, overlapping elbows and you look over, and Eve's very attractive and Maureen's very attractive, and we ended up going out. Maureen and I did date for a while but I completely gave up on her when she got married," Williams says, tongue firmly in cheek. "I felt I was being dumped."

Barry, being the oldest, even had a crush on Florence Henderson and actually took her out once. Florence remembers it wasn't your ordinary date, "I had a date with Barry. We went to the Cocoanut Grove and he wasn't old enough to drive and his brother had to pick us up and drive us."

Eve Plumb and Christopher Knight weren't immune to all those hormones raging around the set either. "Chris and I did go out on a couple of dates," she says. "I had a big crush on him. He's grown up and gotten married to an incredibly wonderful woman, but we've stayed friends and he's still incredibly adorable."

Amazingly, none of this fooling around ever seems to have affected their work on the show—such as if a couple had split up in anger. But maybe it is understandable that none of them ever ended up together, since they spent as much time together as real brothers and sisters and undoubtedly got to see each other's bad sides as well as the good.

THE BRADYS

ROBERT REED

From 1969 to 1974, Robert Reed wasn't just Mike Brady, architect. He was also a cop, Lt. Adam Tobias in *Mannix*. He wasn't the first actor to manage roles in two TV series simultaneously (Nancy Walker did *Rhoda* and *McMillan and Wife* concurrently), but it's hard to imagine two more different characters.

It's fairly well known that Reed was a little contemptuous of Sherwood Schwartz and his role on *The Brady Bunch*, so playing the other role probably gave him the challenge he felt missing in his work on the sitcom.

During the same period, he also appeared on *The Mod Squad, Mission: Impossible*, and *Owen Marshall, Counselor at Law*, expanding his horizons as far as possible.

Reed was born in Highland Park, Illinois on October 19, 1932, the only son of a mink rancher. The family moved to Oklahoma and into cattle ranching when he was six, and he belonged to the 4-H Club. A high school drama class got him interested in acting and he went on to Northwestern University, majoring in drama. Acting became his obsession and he went to London for a year to study at the famous RADA (Royal Academy of Dramatic Arts). He was married briefly and had a daughter, Karen.

He returned to New York and then Chicago, appearing with several theater companies in a number of plays. He migrated to Hollywood, where a role as a lawyer on the popular family show *Father Knows Best* resulted in his being cast as E. G. Marshall's son and law partner on *The Defenders*.

The Defenders ran from 1961 to 1965, and was not only popular, it was critically lauded for addressing ethics and morality along with the law. In fact, Marshall and Reed had some lively discussions during the show's run about issues raised in some of the episodes. Reed told *TV Guide* his feelings about his work: "I couldn't consciously participate in any play that advocated ideas I think are wrong."

After the *The Defenders*, Reed was ready for a change of pace and was under contract to Paramount. The studio planned to do a series version of *Barefoot in the Park*. Reed had taken over the role of Paul on Broadway from Robert Redford, and though Redford got the role in the movie, Reed was supposed to get the TV series. But Paramount shelved the series and he made the pilot for *The Brady Bunch*.

"I thought the show was going to be something else," Reed told *TV Guide*, "that it was going to be more realistic, that we would be real humans. The pilot turned out to be *Gilligan's Island* with kids—full of gags and gimmicks." Somehow, Reed made peace with his role as Mike Brady and even directed a few episodes. Watch out for these, they're the most realistic of the whole series.

Reed's attention to detail was highlighted by Sherwood Schwartz to *TV Guide:* "For instance, in the third show, he said that the kids could not come into his den. In the nineteenth show, the kids did come in, and Bob said, 'But we said the kids couldn't come into the den.' He doesn't realize that by the nineteenth show, people won't remember what we said in the third." Schwartz was wrong about that. When a show develops a cult following as *The Brady Bunch* has, fans revel in just such inconsistencies.

Reed remained rather aloof from the community of actors in Hollywood, which tends to congregate in places like Beverly Hills, Bel Air and Encino. He lived in a beautiful old home in Pasadena, the city of the Tournament of Roses and the Rose Bowl, as well as old money and large, gracious estates. Reed's Mediterranean-style house, built in 1914, was used as a location for the TV movie about Woolworth heiress Barbara Hutton, *Poor Little Rich Girl*.

If anything characterizes Reed's work, it is its variety. He played a senator in a pilot based on Al Capp's cartoon strip, *Li'l Abner*, did intense drama in *Hurry Sundown*,

The City, and *Assignment Munich*, crazy comedy in Rowan and Martin's *The Maltese Bippy*. One of Reed's more interesting appearances was as one of stage legend Gertrude Lawrence's avid suitors in the Julie Andrews film *Star!* In later years he said he couldn't stay away from the filming of the movie even when he wasn't called because he had such admiration for so many excellent people practicing their craft.

Despite his disagreements with Sherwood and Lloyd Schwartz over the direction of *The Brady Bunch*, he never failed to return to the role of Mike Brady in whatever incarnation Schwartz dreamed up. Even in *The Brady Variety Hour*, decked out in shocking pink and Day-Glo orange sequins, he seems to be having a marvelous time.

In fact, Reed became a surrogate father for all the kids on *The Brady Bunch*, and his generosity was legendary. He even took all six kids with him to London on the *QE2*. Barry Williams says, "He *adored* the six of us Brady kids. From day one, he was warm, and very supportive."

Reed had the habit of turning his fellow players into family. Bonnie Hellman, who worked with him on *Nurse* (which filmed in New York City), remembers his generous acting tips and says, "He was like my dad in the city. I had Thanksgiving dinner at his house. We went through stressful times on the show, changing writers and things, and he was always having these parties to cheer everyone up."

Reed passed away at a tragically young 59, on May 12, 1992.

Credits

Feature Films
Bloodlust   1959
Hurry Sundown   1967
Star!   1968
The Love Bug   1968

No Prince for My Cinderella   1978
Prime Target   1991

Theater
Romeo and Juliet
A Month in the Country
Barefoot in the Park—Biltmore Theatre   1964
Deathtrap—The Music Box
Doubles—Broadway and tour
Avanti!—Booth Theatre   1968
The Owl and the Pussycat—national tour
California Suite—national tour
Love Letters—regional theater

Telefilms, Specials, and Series
The Defenders—series   1961–65
Somewhere in Italy, Company B—pilot   1966
Li'l Abner—pilot   1967
The Brady Bunch—series   1969–74
Mannix—series   1969–75
The City—telefilm   1971
Assignment Munich—telefilm   1972
Haunts of the Very Rich—telefilm   1972
Snatched—telefilm   1973
Intersect—pilot   1973
The Man Who Could Talk to Kids—telefilm   1973
Pray for the Wildcats—telefilm   1974
The Secret Night Caller—telefilm   1975
Rich Man, Poor Man—miniseries   1976
Law and Order—telefilm   1976
Lanigan's Rabbi—telefilm   1976
Nightmare in Badham County—telefilm   1976
The Boy in the Plastic Bubble—telefilm   1976
Revenge for a Rape—telefilm   1976
The Love Boat—telefilm   1977
The Brady Bunch Hour—series   1977
Roots—miniseries   1977
SST—Death Flight—telefilm   1977
The Hunted Lady—telefilm   1977

Operation: Runaway—series 1978
Bud and Lou—telefilm 1978
Thou Shalt Not Commit Adultery—telefilm 1978
Mandrake—telefilm 1979
Love's Savage Fury—telefilm 1979
The Seekers—telefilm 1979
Scruples—miniseries 1980
Casino—telefilm 1980
Nurse—telefilm 1980
The Brady Girls Get Married—series 1981
Nurse—series 1981–82
The Brady Girls Get Married—telefilm (re-edited from series) 1981
Death of a Centerfold: The Dorothy Stratton Story—telefilm 1981
International Airport—telefilm 1985
A Very Brady Christmas—telefilm 1988
The Bradys—series 1990

Guest-Starring Roles
The Danny Thomas Show, "Terry Comes Home"
Father Knows Best, "The Impostor"
Men Into Space, "Guidance Control"
Bronco, "Volunteers from Aberdeen"
The Lawman, "Left Hand of the Law"
Dr. Kildare, "The Life Machine," "Toast the Golden Couple," "Wives and Losers," "Welcome Home, Dear Anna," "A Little Child Shall Lead Them," "Hour of Decision," "Aftermath"
Bob Hope Chrysler Theater, "The Admiral"
Hondo, "Hondo and the Superstition Massacre"
Family Affair, "Think Deep"
Ironside, "Light at the End of the Journey"
Journey to the Unknown, "The New People"
Love, American Style, "Love and the Wild Party," "Love and The Vampire," "Love and the Reincarnation"
The Mod Squad, "The Connection"
Mission: Impossible, "The Hit"

Owen Marshall, Counselor at Law, "They've Got to Blame Somebody"

The Man and the City "The City" (pilot)

Chase, "Remote Control"

Harry O, "Accounts Balanced"

Medical Center, "The Fourth Sex"

McCloud, "Fire"

Streets of San Francisco, "The Honorable Profession"

Jigsaw John, "Promise to Kill"

New, Original Wonder Woman, "The Pluto File"

The Wonderful World of Disney, "Kit Carson and the Mountain Men"

Barnaby Jones, "Death Beat"

The Love Boat, "Ex Plus Y," "The Witness," "Friend of the Family," "Seems Like Old Times," "Joint Custody," "Who Killed Maxwell Thorn?"

Lucan, "The Pariah"

Vegas, "The Pageant," "The Usurper"

Fantasy Island, "Vampire"

Hawaii Five-O, "The Pagoda Factor," "Though the Heavens Fell," "Good Help Is Hard to Find"

The Paper Chase, "Once More with Feeling"

Galactica 1980, "Galactica Discovers Earth"

Charlie's Angels, "Angels in Love"

ABC Afterschool Special, "Between Two Loves"

Fantasy Island, "Room and Bard," "Vampire"

Hotel, "Transitions," "Secrets," "Restless Nights"

The Mississippi

Matt Houston, "Stolen"

Cover Up, "A Subtle Seduction"

Finder of Lost Loves, "From the Hearts"

Murder, She Wrote, "Footnote to Murder," "Murder Through the Looking Glass"

Half Nelson, "The Deadly Vase"

Glitter, "Suddenly Innocent"

Crazy Like a Fox, "Just Another Fox in the Crowd"

The Law and Harry McGraw, "Beware the Ides of May"

Hunter, "City of Passion"

Duet, "I Never Played for My Father"
Day by Day, "Bradyvision"
Jake and the Fatman, "Happy Days Are Here Again"

FLORENCE HENDERSON

It's very difficult to reconcile the vivacious, energetic, successful Florence Henderson with her past, which may be the point. "I had a terrible childhood, we were extremely poor. I was the youngest of ten and I had a father who was a sharecropper, a tenant farmer, who struggled with alcoholism all his life," Henderson remembers. "When I got a chance to go to the movies, I didn't want to go see my life, I wanted to go see Jane Powell singing and dancing and Judy Garland and Fred Astaire. I had enough reality at home, and I think that's how people feel about our show. It gave me hope. I knew I could be in show business some day and be just like them, so it gave me a wonderful dream." Her mother was a strong woman, whom Florence credits with her own mental strength and tenacity. She also taught little Florence to sing.

"I was five or six and because we were so poor, my mother would send me to the corner store because she knew that if I would sit on the counter and sing, the people who owned the store would give us some groceries," Henderson remembers. "It was kind of like singing for my supper, which I'm still doing. The numbers I did included 'She'll Be Comin' Round the Mountain When She Comes,' country songs, folk songs, 'The Old Rugged

Cross.'" She also loved making people laugh. "I could have been just as happy being a baggy pants comedian."

Henderson became determined to become a singer and dancer, despite lifelong stage fright, and pains she couldn't explain. In her family, they could never afford to go to doctors. But during her Broadway debut in the musical *Wish You Were Here*, she suffered such pain in her back she finally had it X-rayed and found she had deformed vertebrae. Then, during a performance of *The King and I*, she realized she couldn't hear an instrument in the orchestra which she needed for a musical cue. She suffered with diminishing hearing for years, before going to the right doctor, having it diagnosed and corrected. Later, she was also diagnosed with hypoglycemia.

But like the irrepressible Molly Brown of musical theater, Florence wasn't down yet. She studied at the American Academy of Dramatic Arts. She was spotted by Richard Rodgers while performing in *Wish You Were Here*, and he engaged her to play Laurey in the final *Oklahoma!* national tour.

She has also carved out a successful nightclub singing career over decades, which she gets to do far less often than she'd like. "My favorite type of performing is always when there is a live audience because it's that instant communication, the instant applause and for me, that is ultimately the most satisfying and you know immediately whether you're landing or you're bombing."

She was married for 28 years to theatrical manager Ira Bernstein and they raised four children. Everyone acknowledges that Florence's children have become exceptional adults, despite Florence having another surrogate family, the Brady kids. "It was very natural to treat them as my own children and I still do. I'm sure they all think I'm much too bossy. Sometimes it was difficult for my own children. My children had a lot of problems in school. Sometimes the teachers were extra hard on them . . . I remember once, Lizzie, we were all in Central Park, we were playing, and all these little kids ran up to me and were tugging at me, 'Mrs. Brady, Mrs. Brady,' and Lizzie turned to me and said, 'Mom, tell them we're your real kids.' But they turned out to be wonderful adults."

Florence has married again, her second husband is hypnotherapist John Kappas, and that has given her a second career. "I'm a certified hypnotherapist and I work a lot with terminally ill cancer patients and people facing traumas who need motivation. It's the most exciting, rewarding field and if I were not as busy in my first career as I am, I would do it full time."

Ms. Henderson actively supports several charities, and has served as host of the United Cerebral Palsy telethon. In addition to her show *Country Kitchen*, on the Nashville Network, she occasionally hosts *Nashville Now* and periodically takes her nightclub act on tour around the country.

So what part of her career does this vital, slightly bawdy, still lovely actress remember most fondly? "I loved doing *The Sound of Music* because it satisfied so many people, but the role which no one really knows about is the last show Noël Coward wrote, which is *The Girl Who Came to Supper*, which was based on [the film] *The Prince and the Showgirl* and I played the role that Marilyn Monroe played in the movie and that was a great challenge for me and satisfying. Unfortunately, it was not a big, big hit and didn't run a long time."

Credits

Feature Films
Song of Norway   1980
Shakes the Clown   1992
Naked Gun 33⅓   1992
The Brady Bunch Movie   1995

Theater
Wish You Were Here   1952
Oklahoma!—national tour   1952
The Great Waltz—Los Angeles Civic Light Opera   1953

Fanny—Majestic Theatre   1954–55
The Sound of Music—national tour   1961
The Girl Who Came to Supper   1963
The King and I—LACLO   1965
South Pacific—New York State Theatre   1967
Oh Johnny   1970
Annie Get Your Gun—national tour   1974
Bells Are Ringing—LACLO   1978
Alone Together—La Mirada (CA) Civic Theatre   1989

Telefilms, Specials and Series
General Foods 25th Anniversary Show—special   1954
The Jack Paar Show—series   1957–62
Sing Along—series   1958
Little Women—special   1958
Oldsmobile Music Theater—series   1958
The Today Show—1959–60
Music for a Winter Night—special   1960
The Gershwin Years—special   1961
The Bell Telephone Hour   1964, 1966
The Brady Bunch—series   1969–1974
*Highlights of the Ice Capades: Bell System Family
   Theatre*—special   1970
A World of Love—special   1970
City vs. Country—special   1971
A Salute to TV's 25th Anniversary—special   1972
Broadway My Street—special   1974
The Love Boat—telefilm   1976
The Paul Lynde Halloween Special—special   1976
Bob Hope's Comedy Special from Australia—
   special   1978
The Brady Girls Get Married—series/telefilm   1981
The Brady Brides—series   1981
Country Kitchen—series   1985–1994
Happy Birthday, Hollywood—special   1987
Jay Leno's Family Comedy Hour—special   1987
The Candid Camera Christmas Special—special   1987
A Very Brady Christmas—telefilm   1988

The Mrs. World Pageant—special 1989
Win, Lose or Draw—game 1989
Florence Henderson's Looking Great, Feeling Great—
   video 1990
The Bradys—series 1990
Bradymania!—special 1993
Salute to the '70s—special 1993
The MTV Movie Awards—special 1993
Dave's World—series 1993–94
A Tribute to Moms—1994
The Brady Bunch Home Movies—special 1995

Guest-Starring Roles
The Ed Sullivan Show
Coke Time with Eddie Fisher
The Dean Martin Show
The Jackie Gleason Show
The Jonathan Winters Show
The Hollywood Palace
U.S. Steel Hour, "Huck Finn," "A Family Alliance"
The Voice of Firestone
Car 54, Where Are You?, "I Love Lucille"
The Bing Crosby Show
The Garry Moore Show
I Spy, "The Abbe and the Nymph"
Kraft Music Hall
Operation: Entertainment
The Don Knotts Show
This Is Tom Jones
Medical Center, "Torment"
Good Heavens, "See Jane Run"
The Love Boat, "Divorce Me, Please," "The Remake,"
   "The Successor," "The Return of Annabelle," "Affair
   on Demand," "Who Killed Maxwell Thorn?"
Hart to Hart, "Hartland Express"
Fantasy Island, "The Sailor," "Pentagram," "My Mommy
   the Swinger"

Police Squad!, "Rendezvous at Big Gulch (Terror in the Neighborhood)"*

Alice

Glitter, "A Minor Miracle"

Finder of Lost Loves, "Forgotten Melodies"

Cover Up, "Healthy, Wealthy and Dead"

New Love, American Style, "Love and the Piano Teacher"

Murder She Wrote, "Death Stalks the Big Top"

ABC Afterschool Special, "Just a Regular Kid: An AIDs Story"

It's Garry Shandling's Show, "The Schumokers Go to Hollywood"

Day by Day, "Bradyvision"

Free Spirit

The Mommies

Roseanne

Dave's World

Books

One-Minute Bible Stories: New Testament, Florence Henderson and Shari Lewis, 1986

A Little Cooking, A Little Talking and a Whole Lot of Fun, Florence Henderson 1988

*All episodes of *Police Squad!* had two titles, the first on the screen and the second, the announcer's voice-over. Neither had anything to do with the episode's contents.

ANN B. DAVIS

Bitten by the acting bug after seeing her brother perform in *Oklahoma!*, Ann B. Davis switched her studies from premed at the University of Michigan to drama. The girl from Schenectady, New York, crisscrossed the country in little theater until making it at last to Hollywood, where a friend of a friend arranged an audition for the role of Bob Cummings' girl Friday on a new TV show.

She got the part of Charmaine "Shultzy" Schultz on *The Bob Cummings Show* and was nominated for four Emmys for it—she won two. She also got her star on the Hollywood Walk of Fame. Today, she says her luck was because "I was in on the ground floor of television. I always played the underdog and I think that was one of my appeals. Because everybody is an underdog to somebody. And because I had writers behind me, I could say all the things people think of to say . . . later."

So she was already a familiar figure in the nation's living rooms when she went on to play a phys. ed. teacher in *The John Forsythe Show*. Forsythe was a fish-out-of-water headmaster of a posh San Francisco girls' school, but this show never gained the popularity of his previous run with *Bachelor Father,* so Ann B. hit the road again.

When Florence Henderson, a musical comedy actress rather than a comedienne, was cast as Carol Brady, it became clear that the comedic focus of *The Brady Bunch* would shift away from the wacky wife to the housekeeper. And Sherwood Schwartz didn't just want an Ann B. Davis type for the part, he wanted the original.

Aside from her extensive television work, Ann B. appeared in several films, including playing an Alice-type housekeeper in the Doris Day–Rock Hudson comedy, *Lover Come Back*, and appeared in *A Man Called Peter, Pepe, All Hands on Deck*, and *Naked Gun 33⅓.*

Ann B. joined an Episcopalian community in 1976, but hits the road every now and again. She recently joined the national company of the musical *Crazy for You* and performed in the show on Broadway.

According to Andrew J. Edelstein and France Lovece's *The Brady Bunch Book*, Ann B. created a whole backstory for her character as Alice. Drawing partly from her life, she decided that Alice had a twin sister (as did Ann B.) and that they were orphaned early in life (not like Ann B.). Alice took whatever jobs she could get to put her sister through college, and found she enjoyed being a housekeeper/nursemaid.

Incidentally, no two actors are allowed by their unions to use the same name. The reason Ann B. Davis had to use her middle initial is that there was already an Ann Davis, an actress who made her stage debut in 1909 and retired from the stage in 1931; she passed away in 1961.

But our Ann B. is very much alive, and appears in 1995's *The Brady Bunch Movie* in a tongue-in-cheek cameo as a truck driver named "Shultzy." And her reaction to all the Brady fame? "I travel a great deal. To be recognized on the street in Nairobi can really clear your sinuses. It's true—Sydney, Australia—everyplace I go."

Several years ago, she said, "I would like to point out that never, in the 22 years we've been on the air, have we ever gotten a good review. However, we are still on the air because you like us."

Credits

Feature Films
A Man Called Peter 1955
Pepe 1960
All Hands on Deck 1961
Lover, Come Back 1961
Naked Gun 33⅓: The Final Insult 1994
The Brady Bunch Movie 1995

Theater
The Matchmaker
Auntie Mame
Blithe Spirit
Funny Girl
Once Upon a Mattress—Phoenix Theatre
No, No, Nanette—national tour
The Nearlyweds
Rockers
Crazy for You—Shubert Theatre and national tour

Telefilms, Specials and Series
The Bob Cummings Show (a.k.a. *Love That Bob*)—
   series   1955–59
The Keefe Brasselle Show—series   1963
The John Forsythe Show—series   1965–66
The Brady Bunch—series   1969–74
The Brady Bunch Hour—series   1977
The Brady Brides—series   1981
The Bradys—series   1990

Guest-Starring Roles
The Colgate Comedy Hour
Art Linkletter's House Party
Lux Video Theatre, "The Wayward Saint"
The Perry Como Show
The Arthur Murray Party
Wagon Train, "The Countess Baranof Story"
McKeever and the Colonel, "Too Many Sergeants"
The Bob Hope Chrysler Theatre, "Wake Up, Darling"
The Dating Game
Love, American Style, "Love and the Trip"
The Love Boat
Day by Day, "Bradyvision"
The People Next Door
Hi Honey, I'm Home

BARRY WILLIAMS

Barry Williams became an actor because he lived on the same block as Peter Graves. The youngster was so impressed with his neighbor, who at the time was starring in *Fury*, he actually decided that's what he wanted to do. And, miraculously, he not only did it, he even had a guest-starring role on *Mission: Impossible*, starring Peter Graves.

It wasn't easy. Barry had to survive the rigors of being mascot for his brothers' gang and his parents' extreme lack of enthusiasm, but he took an acting class, did a documentary, got an agent, and soon, he landed a Sears commercial and then went on to guest roles in TV series.

In his book, *Growing Up Brady*, he says that after a role on the Ben Gazzara show *Run for Your Life*, "for about six months, if a series needed a runaway/punk/delinquent/ from a dysfunctional family/with a heart of gold, it was me." After several years, the roles started to not only become more varied, they expanded. On the fabled *Mission: Impossible*, Williams got to play a young Middle Eastern king in the middle of a power struggle, who has to escape his country disguised as a gypsy *girl*.

He went to a cattle call for the role of Greg in *The Brady Bunch*, a job that was more dependent on the matching of the three boys than with their credits. Still, after a round of auditions and interviews, he had the part.

"We had a gas," Williams says. "I loved working on the show. Paramount Studios was our neighborhood and our neighbors were the casts of the other shows filming on the lot—*The Odd Couple*, *Star Trek*, *Mannix*, *Mission: Impossible*, and *Happy Days*. It was, like, standing at the commissary between Mr. Phelps and Mr. Spock."

As the oldest of the six Brady kids, he was the natural leader, but he says, "I never paid a whole lot of attention to upholding an image. I wanted to be on the cutting edge and I think I was fairly successful, at least with the bell bottoms. One of the tougher things is this whole teen idol thing. It's very, very transitory. Mostly you appeal to 10- to 14-year-old girls and you have to project a very innocent image."

But every hiatus, the transition back to regular life wasn't easy. He says, "Kids would mostly try to avoid us. We were famous, we were on television, and you'd walk into the classroom and they were kind of uncomfortable with it. I was uncomfortable with them because I wasn't hanging with my own friends. We were in kind of an adult world on the set and those were the people I knew the best and could relate to."

But those relationships were sometimes in transition, Barry remembers, "We had a lot of trouble separating fantasy from reality. It would be hard for us not to. We were together as a group sometimes more than we were with our own families. So we had to learn to either love each other or hate each other. We did a little of both. First I set my sights on Carol Brady, but really, I had a relationship with Maureen McCormick through many of the years, off again/on again. We were actors and not really related. When the cameras stopped rolling, sometimes we started."

After *The Brady Bunch* was over, Williams was signed to star in the national tour of *Pippin*, but when that year was up, he was back playing Greg Brady again on *The Brady Bunch Hour* and the subsequent reunions, specials, series, and assorted appearances. He went on a national tour to promote his autobiography of his *Brady* years, *Growing Up Brady* (written with Chris Kreski), which he also calls, "For Whom the Bell Bottoms Toll."

He has returned to the stage (mostly regional theater) again and again, and continues to pursue his acting career in Southern California. His appearance as the manager who rejects Johnny Bravo in the new *Brady Bunch* movie is especially fun.

Credits

Feature Films
Wild in the Streets   1968
The Wilderness Family Part 2   1978
Fresh Horses   1988
The Brady Bunch Movie   1995

Theater
Pippin—Imperial Theatre and national tour   1974–75
Oklahoma!
West Side Story
The Music Man
I Love My Wife
They're Playing Our Song
Wait Until Dark
I Do! I Do!
Promises, Promises
Movie Star—Westwood Playhouse   1982
Romance, Romance—Helen Hayes Theatre   1988–89
Slay It with Music—Actors Outlet (Off-Broadway)   1989
City of Angels—tour   1992
The Paisley Convertible—Goodfield, Illinois   1992
Man of La Mancha   1994

Telefilms, Specials, and Series
General Hospital—soap   1969, 1984
The Brady Bunch—series   1969–74
The Shameful Secrets of Hastings Corners—pilot   1970
The Brady Kids—animated series   1972–74
The Brady Bunch Variety Hour—special   1976
The Brady Bunch Hour—variety series   1977
The Brady Girls Get Married—telefilm   1981
The Brady Brides—series   1981
A Very Brady Christmas—special   1988
The Bradys—series   1990
Bradymania!—special   1993

Salute to the '70s—special   1993
The Brady Bunch Home Movies—special   1995

Guest-Starring Roles
Run for Your Life, "Hoodlums on Wheels"
The Invaders, "The Mutation"
Dragnet, "The Christmas Story"
That Girl, "7½, Part I"
Adam 12, "A Dead Cop Can't Help Anyone"
Gomer Pyle, U.S.M.C., "?"
The Mod Squad, "The Guru"
Here Come the Brides, "A Kiss Just for You"
The Andy Griffith Show
Lancer, "Blood Rock"
It Takes a Thief, "A Matter of Grey Matter" (2-part)
Mission: Impossible, "Gitano"
Marcus Welby, M.D., "The Chemistry of Hope"
Three's Company, "Up in the Air"
American Bandstand
Police Woman, "Generation of Evil"
Highway to Heaven
Murder, She Wrote, "Night of the Headless Horseman"

Books
Growing Up Brady, Barry Williams with Chris Kreski
(HarperCollins, 1992)

MAUREEN McCORMICK

Maureen McCormick's pre-*Brady* background is similar to Barry Williams' (except she didn't live near Peter Graves). Like Barry, she was the youngest child in the family, and started on the path to Hollywood early. In her case, she won a beautiful baby contest when she was six, and soon had an agent. She made her stage debut at age seven at the La Jolla Playhouse.

But it was her voice that proved to be the real entree for McCormick. She was chosen to record the words for all the Mattel talking dolls, including Chatty Cathy, and she did the voice of Peppermint Patty in the *Peanuts* animated specials. She performed in over 50 commercials (including getting to poke the Pillsbury Doughboy) and branched into series television with roles on *Bewitched* (as a juvenile witch), *Honey West, My Three Sons,* and others.

Like the other kids, Maureen participated in the cattle call for *The Brady Bunch* and grew up as America watched. She had the best singing voice and it's due in large part to her talent that the Brady Kids made as many recordings as they did. In his book *Growing Up Brady*, Barry Williams describes putting together the first Christmas album. Williams recalls that the record's producer never bothered to check anyone's ability or vocal range, he just arbitrarily assigned songs. Barry was assigned "O Holy Night," a difficult song for even the most seasoned professional. Williams did his best, which wasn't good enough. The engineer called in Maureen. "She actually had a pretty good voice, and since the song was in her range, *she* tackled the more treacherous first half, and I simply chimed in halfway through. With the two of us singing, it was only half awful—*my* half."

Maureen did a number of guest shots on TV shows after *The Brady Bunch*, and was frequently seen on both *Fantasy Island* and *The Love Boat*. She appeared in several films, most of the *Brady* reunion vehicles (she missed *The Bradys* because she was having a baby), and is currently launching her country western singing career with a new album.

Credits

Feature Films
The Boys   1961
The Arrangement   1969
Pony Express Rider   1976
Moonshine County Express   1977
Casey's Shadow   1978
Take Down   1979
Skatetown, USA   1979
The Idolmaker   1980
Texas Lightning   1987
Return to Horror High   1987

Theater
Wind It Up and It Breaks—La Jolla Playhouse   1964
McCarthy—Odyssey Theatre
Peter Pan—San Bernardino Civic Light Opera

Telefilms, Specials and Series
The Brady Bunch—series   1969–74
The Brady Kids—animated series   1972–74
Gibbsville: The Turning Point of Jim Malloy—telemovie   1975
The Brady Bunch Variety Hour—special   1976
The Brady Bunch Hour—variety series   1977
A Vacation in Hell—telemovie   1979
Runaways—telemovie   1979
When, Jenny? When?—special   1980
The Brady Girls Get Married—telefilm   1981

The Brady Brides—series   1981
A Very Brady Christmas—special   1988
Faculty Lounge—pilot
Bradymania!—special   1993
Salute to the '70s—special   1993

Guest-Starring Roles
Bewitched, "And Something Makes Three," "Trick or
   Treat"
The Farmer's Daughter, "Why Don't They Ever Pick Me?"
Honey West, "In the Bag"
Camp Runamuck, "Tomboy"
I Dream of Jeannie, "My Master, the Doctor"
My Three Sons, "Ernie the Bluebeard"
Marcus Welby, M.D., "The Day After Forever"
Happy Days, "Crusin' "
Harry O, "Secret Games"
Joe Forrester, "Bus Station"
Streets of San Francisco, "No Minor Voices"
Gibbsville, "All the Young Girls"
Delvecchio, "One Little Indian"
The Love Boat, "First Time Out," "Winner Take Love,"
   "Gopher's Engagement," "First Voyage, Last Voyage,"
   "The Christmas Presence"
Nancy Drew Mysteries, "Nancy Drew's Love Match"
Fantasy Island, "Beauty Contest," "Aphrodite,"
   "Reprisal," "The Sisters," "Best Seller," "The Tomb,"
   "Roller Derby Queen," "Dr. Jekyll and Miss Hyde,"
   "The Boxer"
Vegas, "The Pageant"
Lou Grant, "Sweep"
New Love, American Style, "Love and the F.M. Doctor"
Day by Day, "A Brady Vision"

CHRISTOPHER
KNIGHT

Like Susan Olsen, Chris Knight came from a showbiz family. He was born in New York but raised in Los Angeles, where his father ran a small theater group. His first work was in commercials, and he did dozens of them, including one for Cheerios, and appeared in several television series.

He says he didn't have the happiest home life and the Brady household was a nice escape. Chris and Mike Lookinland were best pals, making model rockets and terrorizing the Paramount backlot and being teased by Barry Williams.

"There's a lot of pressure on you as an actor—there's a lot of pressure on anyone growing up as an adolescent. I'm not exactly Peter Brady but I didn't have a problem."

Chris tried to keep his career going post-*Brady*, but it was spotty at best. In 1987, he got a new opportunity. "I removed myself from the acting community. I was fortunate to have a friend who had a company who invited me to work for him, and I'm now working for a new company, as an executive in the sales department at New Image Industries. He took a leave from that job to do *The Bradys*, but the series was short-lived.

Chris designed an interactive geography computer program featuring the Brady kids and has a cameo in *The Brady Bunch Movie* (look for him in the high school cafeteria scene).

Credits

Feature Films
Studs Lonigan   1960
The Narrow Chute   1970
The Brady Bunch Movie   1995

Theater
Letting Go
Accommodations
The Mousetrap
Mrs. Dally Has a Lover
A Life In the Theatre

Telefilms, Specials, and Series
The Brady Bunch—series   1969–74
Joe's World—series   1979–80
The Brady Kids—animated series   1972–74
The Brady Bunch Variety Hour—special   1976
The Brady Bunch Hour—variety series   1977
Diary of a Hitchhiker—telefilm   1979
Valentine Magic on Love Island—pilot   1980
The Brady Girls Get Married—telefilm   1981
The Brady Brides—series   1981
A Very Brady Christmas—special   1988
The Bradys—series   1990
Bradymania!—special   1993
Salute to the '70s—special   1993
Good Girls Don't—telefilm   1993
The Brady Bunch Home Movies—special   1995

Guest-Starring Roles
Bonanza
Gunsmoke
ABC Afterschool Special, "Sara's Summer of the Swans"
Mannix, "Coffin for a Clown"
One Day at a Time
Little House on the Prairie
CHiPs, "Family Crisis"

Happy Days, "Be My Valentine"
The Love Boat, "Baby Sister"
On the Television, "A Not So Very Brady Rockin' New
   Year's Eve"
Day by Day, "Bradyvision"

EVE PLUMB

   Like several of the other Brady kids, Eve Plumb grew
up in a showbiz family. She was raised in Burbank, her
father a record producer and agent and her mother an
actress and ballet teacher. Eve's first commercial was for
a fabric softener, and she got work in TV shortly after that.
She was cast in a pilot for *The Barbara Rush Show,* a
sitcom about a woman struggling to put her husband
through medical school by working as a public stenog-
rapher and raising three kids. The show was written by
Barbara Avedon, a sitcom veteran from *Bewitched,* who
would later go on to co-create *Cagney and Lacey.*
   Between that and *The Brady Bunch,* Eve made dozens
of commercials and guested on a number of TV shows.
Even with the weird schedule of making a TV series, she
managed to do extremely well in school and became a fine
horsewoman.
   After *Brady,* Eve Plumb got rave notices for one of the
first really hard-hitting TV movies about teenage prosti-
tution, *Dawn: Portrait of a Teenage Runaway* in 1976.
She's worked off and on since then, doing all of the various *Brady* reunion shows except the variety hour. She
even did a cameo appearance in the Chicago company of
The Real Live Brady Bunch.

Eve played Mrs. Noah in a documentary spoof called *And God Spoke* in 1994, and she is venturing into a new field, stand-up comedy, with L.A.'s premier improvisation troupe, the Groundlings, and she worked with Florence Henderson again on a Saturday morning show, *Superfudge*.

Credits

Feature Films
I'm Gonna Git You, Sucka   1988
And God Spoke   1994

Theater
Slumber Party
Your Very Own TV Show
South Pacific—Bucks County Playhouse   1991
The Real Live Brady Bunch—Annoyance Theatre   1991
Charles Manson: The Musical

Telefilms, Specials, and Series
The Barbara Rush Show—pilot   1965
In Name Only—telefilm   1969
The Brady Bunch—series   1969–74
The House on Greenapple Road—telefilm   1970
The Brady Kids—animated series   1972–74
The Brady Bunch Variety Hour—special   1976
Dawn: Portrait of a Teenage Runaway—telefilm   1976
Alexander: The Other Side of Dawn—telefilm   1977
Telethon—telefilm   1977
Little Women—telefilm   1978
Secrets of Three Hungry Wives—telefilm   1978
The Brady Brides—series   1981
The Brady Girls Get Married—telefilm   1981
The Night the Bridge Fell Down—telefilm   1983
A Very Brady Christmas—special   1988
The Bradys—series   1990
Yesterday Today—pilot   1992
Bradymania!—special   1993

Salute to the '70s—special 1993
The Brady Bunch Home Movies—special 1995

Guest-Starring Roles

The Smothers Brothers Show, " 'Twas the Week Before Christmas"
The Big Valley, "Hide the Children," "Brother Love," "Explosion"
The Virginian
Mannix
It Takes a Thief, "The Radomir Miniature"
Lassie
Family Affair, "Christmas Came a Little Early"
Lancer, "The Heart of Pony Alice"
Here's Lucy, "Lucy and Donny Osmond"
ABC Afterschool Special, "Sara's Summer of the Swans"
Tales of the Unexpected, "The Force of Evil"
New Adventures of Wonder Woman, "The Pied Piper"
Insight, "Is Anybody Listening?"
The Love Boat, "Gopher the Rebel"
Greatest Heroes of the Bible, "The Story of Noah"
Fantasy Island, "Seance," "Swimmer," "Elizabeth's Baby"
The Love Boat, "Honeymoon Pressure," "Command Performance"
One Day at a Time
The Facts of Life, "Best Sister"
Masquerade, "Spying Down to Mexico"
Murder, She Wrote, "Jessica Behind Bars"
Lois & Clark, "Illusions of Grandeur"
On the Television, "A Not So Very Brady Rockin' New Year's Eve"

MIKE LOOKINLAND

Mike's career started in commercials. He was born in Utah, but his father moved the family to Los Angeles to take a job in the L.A. public school system. His mother was also a teacher and his older sister and younger brother all did modeling and commercials as well as a little television (Todd Lookinland appears in the would-be pilot episode, "Kelly's Kids"). Mike did a Band-Aid commercial, a Cheerios spot, a yogurt commercial, and a toy commercial, among others, before being cast in *The Brady Bunch*.

He enjoyed working on the show, especially because there were six kids in the show. "In retrospect, it was really important for us to have peers to play with," he says, "because we were kids. We spent a lot of our time working, but when we weren't working, we were either in school or fooling around. You know, climbing ladders and running around the backlot."

He worked a little during the series and in Universal's big disaster movie, *The Towering Inferno*, and recorded a single record, but his career faded in his high school years.

Later, he moved to working behind the camera. "After years and years of wandering, I found my niche." He was a camera assistant on Stephen King's *The Stand* and did a cameo in the miniseries.

He's a loyal Deadhead. "I've seen the Grateful Dead 96 times."

Credits

Feature Films
The Towering Inferno   1974

Telefilms, Specials and Series
The Brady Bunch—series   1969–74

Dead Men Tell No Tales—telemovie 1971
The Point—animated special 1971
The Brady Kids—animated series 1972–74
The Brady Bunch Variety Hour—special 1976
The Brady Bunch Hour—variety series 1977
The Brady Girls Get Married—telefilm 1981
The Brady Brides—series 1981
A Very Brady Christmas—special 1988
Bradymania!—special 1993
The Stand—miniseries 1994
The Brady Bunch Home Movies—special 1995

Guest-Starring Roles
Funny Face
American Bandstand
The Wonderful World of Disney, "Bayou Boy"
Day by Day, "Bradyvision"

SUSAN OLSEN

"I want to clear up the rumor that I OD'd and I'm dead. I'm not dead, it just seems that way. It's Buffy on *Family Affair* who overdosed and because we looked alike, people think it was me." Susan Olsen wasn't kidding when she said this recently. Today, she's a woman with a good self-image, a wide variety of talents, and a sense of humor.

If you want to see a *Brady*-vintage Susan Olsen without her Buffy hairdo, rent the Elvis Presley film *The Trouble With Girls*. She sings "If You Wore a Tulip," and is adorable.

Susan Olsen grew up in Santa Monica, in a house full of showbiz folks. Her siblings, ranging wildly in age, all worked in the business, either in modeling, television, or films. "I began acting at 14 months," Susan says. "At 13 months, I was searching for work. As luck would have it, I got sort of discovered for commercials when I was 14 months old and my mother took me out of the business when I was about three, so I thought I'd lead a normal life. But as luck would have it, I was in kindergarten at age five and I got picked by the talent scouts, so I got like a second chance."

The most pragmatic of all the Brady kids, Susan seems to have taken it all in stride. "I feel like my family, they weren't like *The Brady Bunch*, I mean we didn't spend entire weeks looking for my doll. But I don't think anybody would necessarily want their family to be exactly like *The Brady Bunch*, but a good family is certainly comparable. I liked my family, I was proud to be in my family, and I certainly thought we were cooler than the Bradys."

If you think child actors can't be well-adjusted, just listen to Olsen: "It was not really a childhood, but I was the type of child that I wanted that. I would get to have my normal life during hiatus and I would go to regular school with my regular friends and do all the regular things kids do, and by the time hiatus was over, I was very bored. I wanted to go back and work. I enjoyed working. I thought of it as a job, a profession."

Everyone in the cast agrees that Susan was less like her character than the rest of them. She remembers, "If you really think about it, a lot of the things that Cindy said, they were cute, but if you think about it, it's almost as if she was retarded. There were a lot of dumb things. And I would have to go back to public school. I was always so grateful the show was on Fridays, that way, people would forget what happened over the weekend, but I'd go to public school on Mondays and they'd say, 'You're so stupid, I can't believe what you said.'"

She came back for about half of the Brady reunions. She avoided the others because of a little ambivalence about being forever associated with one role. "*The Brady Bunch* was like a tattoo that wouldn't wash off," she says. Of course, some of us wanted to move on and some of us chose to stay away from *Brady* adventures, and for me, sometimes I get a little sick of it, but I make the best of it. When I became an adult and wanted to get back into acting, it became extremely limiting. Back then, the show really wasn't all that respected and the typecasting made it virtually impossible to get out on auditions."

Olsen's career since *The Brady Bunch* has been mostly as a graphic artist. Her sneaker designs were bought by Converse and Glow All-Stars hit the market. She silk-screens T-shirts and, most recently, assembled all the home movies the Brady kids shot with the movie cameras given to them by Robert Reed. With them, she produced a TV special, *The Brady Bunch Home Movies*, which aired in 1995.

Credits

Feature Films
The Trouble With Girls   1969

Telefilms, Specials, and Series
The Brady Bunch—series   1969–74
The Brady Kids—animated series   1972–74
The Brady Bunch Variety Hour—special   1976
The Brady Bunch Hour—variety series   1977
The Brady Girls Get Married—telefilm   1981
Bradymania!—special   1993
The Brady Bunch Home Movies—special   1995

Guest-Starring Roles
Ironside
Gunsmoke, "Abelia," "A Man Called Smith"
Julia

American Bandstand
The Wonderful World of Disney, "The Boy Who Stole the
   Elephant"

A.B. (AFTER BRADY)

Like the prior show Sherwood Schwartz did, *Gilligan's Island*, there was little hint as the cast parted for hiatus that they wouldn't be renewed. They were still reasonably successful, merchandising for the show was hot, the kids were touring with a musical act and making albums.

Because TV shows usually finish shooting in March and don't know about renewal sometimes until May, a cancellation can be a real blow, with no chance for a final episode, no chance to say good-bye, no chance to get together one last time. But the network lowered the boom without any notice.

Considering the group all regarded each other as family, this must have been truly a shock. And since the show's audience also regarded the Bradys as family, they missed them.

But it wasn't long before the Bradys were again everywhere in syndication. And on Saturday mornings, and then in prime time again.

The Brady Kids

Animated children's show
ABC Saturdays 10:30 A.M.—1972–74 (22 episodes)
Regulars: Williams, McCormick, Knight, Plumb,
   Lookinland, Olsen

The kids (with the live-action series actors supplying the voices) on adventures minus adults and plus an assortment of magical animals.

The Brady Bunch Variety Hour

Comedy/variety special
ABC Sunday 7–8 P.M.—November 28, 1976
Regulars: Reed, Henderson, Davis, Williams, McCormick,
   Knight, Geri Reischl (as Jan Brady), Lookinland, Olsen
Guests: Donny and Marie Osmond, Tony Randall

A variety show with musical guests and sketches picking up the family from where the series left off. Created and produced by Sid and Marty Krofft of puppet fame, who were at the time producing *Donny and Marie*. If the Osmonds could have a show, why not the Bradys? If the Osmonds had an ice rink, why couldn't the Bradys have a swimming pool? And if we have a guest on *Donny and Marie* one week, why can't they guest on *The Brady Bunch Hour* the next?

   This show has been run several times by the Nickelodeon cable network and is a delight of bell bottoms, Day-Glo orange and pink. Mike gives up his career to manage the family band and they all move to the beach. Seriously, everybody's giving it all they've got, and it's more fun than a potato sack race!

The Brady Bunch Hour

Comedy/variety series
ABC Sundays, Mondays, Wednesdays, and Fridays,
January–May 1977 (8 episodes)
Regulars: Reed, Henderson, Davis, Williams, McCormick,
Knight, Geri Reischl (as Jan Brady), Lookinland, Olsen,
Rip Taylor, The Krofftette Dancers, The Water Follies
Swimmers
Guests: Farrah Fawcett-Majors, Lee Majors, Kaptain Kool
and the Kongs,* Milton Berle, Tina Turner, Vincent
Price, Redd Foxx, Rick Dees, the kids from *What's
Happening!!*, Paul Williams, Lynn Anderson

Each show was essentially a repeat of the previous one with
different guests and slightly wider bell bottoms, a few more
sequins and feathers, and more blinding colors.

The Brady Brides

Telefilm re-edited into a series
NBC Fridays 8:00 P.M.
February–April 1981
Regulars: Reed, Henderson, Davis, Williams, McCormick,
Knight, Plumb, Lookinland, Olsen, Jerry Houser, Ron
Kuhlman

Originally shot as a two-hour TV movie, moments before it
was to air on February 6, 1981, CBS pulled it, told Sherwood Schwartz to re-edit it as four half-hour shows, add six
more, and voilà! A series!

Nothing is generally that simple, and this certainly
wasn't. The original culminated in Jan and Marcia's double
wedding and house-hunting, and now what do you do with
them? The problem was never solved, the time slot was
wrong and the show died a fairly painful death.

*And you thought music group names were ridiculous today!

A Very Brady Christmas

Telemovie
Sunday, December 17, 1988
Regulars: Reed, Henderson, Davis, Williams, McCormick,
Knight, Plumb, Lookinland, Jennifer Runyon (as Cindy
Brady), Houser, Kuhlman

Like a phoenix rising from the ashes, the Bradys reassem-
bled for what became the second-highest-rated TV movie
of the year. The plot was simple: Mike and Carol decide to
have *everyone* to the house for Christmas. Along the way,
we discover the lumps and bumps in the Brady kids' mar-
riages, meet the next generation, and save Mike from a construction mishap.

The Bradys

Limited Series
CBS Fridays 8:00 P.M.
February–March 1990
Regulars: Reed, Henderson, Davis, Williams, McCormick,
Knight, Plumb, Lookinland, Olsen

Again the network mentality: if one *Brady* TV movie can
haul in 39 percent of the people watching TV, America
must want more. CBS first decided to do two 2-hour tele-
movies, then decided to break it apart into four shows, add
two, and get six, which might make folks long for a series.
It's not that they didn't learn from the last debacle—that
was a different network!

This unlovable series begins with Bobby becoming a par-
aplegic in a racing accident and gets more depressing from
there.

The Real Live Brady Bunch

Live theatrical production
Chicago, Los Angeles
1990–1991

The brainchild of two sisters, Jill and Faith Soloway, who wondered what a TV show would look like on stage, *The Real Live Brady Bunch* was a sellout for over a year at the Annoyance Theatre in Chicago. Each show consisted of a real episode of *The Brady Bunch* (a different one every two weeks).

The Brady Bunch Movie

Feature Film
Paramount Studios, 1995

Cast: Shelley Long . . . . .Carol Brady
  Gary Cole. . . . . Mike Brady
  Christopher Daniel Barnes . . . . Greg Brady
  Christine Taylor. . . . . Marcia Brady
  Paul Sutera. . . . . Peter Brady
  Jennifer Elise Cox . . . . Jan Brady
  Jesse Lee . . . . .Bobby Brady
  Olivia Hack. . . . . Cindy Brady
  Henriette Mantel. . . . . .Alice

This film features a startling re-creation of the original series cast (just close your eyes when Gary Cole says a line and you will *swear* it's Robert Reed). The house is the same, the Formica is the same, the Astroturf is the same. The plot is an amalgam of many classic episodes. But it's 1995, and since the Bradys were out of touch with the '70s even when living in them, this works on many levels. It's really fun to think that the grungy kids in today's Westdale High would think that Marcia, despite her retro look, morals, and manner, is still the hottest girl around.

One of the main things that changed was that the long-suffering actual residents of the Bradys' house said thanks-but-no-thanks this time. Because the original Brady house's owner had had enough of filming, an exact replica was constructed in front of a completely different house. This was also done for the sequel.

❀

Parodies and tributes to the Bradys abound on television, including an episode of *Day by Day*, which stars Christopher Daniel Barnes imagining he's a Brady (and then he was—in the movie), Jay Leno's parody of the show's opening credits during the Simpson trial, called, of course, "The O. J. Bunch," with the dream team and prosecutors occupying the squares—and Rosa Lopez as Alice.

Original licensed merchandise was plentiful for *The Brady Bunch*, and it is now well beyond the price range of normal humans.

❀

Thanks to the new movies, the Bradys live on, complete with weird clothes, old-fashioned values, an empty doghouse, no toilet in the bathroom, and astroturf for lawns. And just like in the movies, they're the nicest family on the block.

INDEXES

EPISODE INDEX

Numbers refer to episode numbers, not page numbers

WRITER & DIRECTOR INDEX

Numbers refer to episode numbers, not page numbers
Credits are in the order they appear on the screen
Objects are closer than they appear

207

GUEST STAR INDEX

Numbers refer to episode numbers, not page numbers